WHY 2K? A Chronological Study of the (Y2K) Millennium Bug:
Why, when and how did Y2K become a critical issue for businesses?

Edna O.F. Reid

Universal Publishers/UPUBLISH.COM
1999

Publisher Data www.upublish.com/books/reid.htm

Reid, Edna O.F.

WHY 2K? A chronological study of the (Y2K) Millennium Bug: Why, when and how did Y2K became a critical issue for businesses? /Edna O.F. Reid.
vi,170 p.; cm.

Includes bibliographical references (p82-93) and index.
1. Year 2000 date conversion (Computer systems). 2. Software maintenance. 3. Diffusion of innovations. 4. Technological innovations. I. Title

ISBN 1-58112-770-7
Universal Publishers/uPUBLISH.com

Author's Dedication

This book is dedicated to my family, Singapore Friends, and colleagues at Nanyang Business School, NTU, Singapore. A special dedication is extended to Leroy, Sharnita, Nestor, Ruth Ferguson (my mother), and Abelardo Valida (my husband).

Author's Disclaimer

I have tried my very best to provide accurate information. Nevertheless, I am advising you that I make no representations or warranties with respect to the contents and specifically disclaim any implied warranties or merchantability or fitness for any particular purpose.

SITDRAC (Singapore IT Dispute Resolution Advisory Committee)

SITDRAC comprises key representatives from:

National Computer Board (NCB)
Singapore Federation of the Computer Industry (SFCI)
Microcomputer Trade Association of Singapore (MTAS)
Singapore Computer Society (SCS)
Information Technology Management Association (ITMA)
Singapore Mediation Centre (SMC)
Singapore International Arbitration Centre (SIAC).

It is set up as an advisory committee under NCB, SMC and SIAC. SITDRAC advises on issues, practices and matters relating to IT disputes.

SITDRAC's Disclaimer

This study was commissioned by SITDRAC. The materials contained herein represent solely the work and views of the author. SITDRAC disclaims all liabilities, obligations and warranties of any nature whatsoever.

WHY 2K? A Chronological Study of the (Y2K) Millennium Bug

Table

Figure

References   82

Appendices

Index   168

WHY 2K? A Chronological Study of the (Y2K) Millennium Bug

Chapter 1: Introduction and Research Approach

The Year 2000 (Y2K) computer problem is globally considered as one of this century's most critical issues so much so that the world community has joined forces to resolve the problem. The US President's Council on Year 2000 Conversion, the Dutch Millennium Platform, Singapore's National Computer Board (NCB), and the UK Government Action 2000 initiative have asked associations, governments and enterprises to share their Y2K related resources with the wider community. In addition, legislators, government authorities, and industry leaders are working to support the resolution of the problem and ensure public safety.

Nature of the Problem

The Y2K problem concerns the widespread practice of storing calendar year dates in two-digit form. Until 1989, all the standards followed in creating computer programs stated that only two digits "the last two" would be used to identify the year (deJager & Bergeon, 1997 p vi). For example, the year 1988 is stored as 88. At the end of the twentieth century, many software applications will stop working or create erroneous results when the year switches from 1999 to 2000 (Jones, 1998 p1). Since many applications use dates for time-dependent calculations, the ones involved in long-term mortgage or insurance calculations have already produced problems.

According to Y2K consultants deJager and Bergeon, the Year 2000 problem is a series of problems, some involving computer software, some involving computer hardware, some involving data, and all involving large amounts of money to fix. Although the problem is largely technical in nature, it poses serious threats because of the domino effect. The domino effect highlights how today's businesses have developed into an integrated network of dependency through their information systems (IS). This network involves a tangled web of business interrelationships that exist among enterprises and third parties such as their suppliers, customers, financial service providers, government agencies, and telecommunication providers (Meador & Freeman, 1997).

Another aspect of the problem is embedded chips (www.year2000.com/archive/NFexperience-1.html). Embedded chips are "embedded" computer chips used to control, monitor or assist the operation of machinery, equipment, or plant (World, 1998). Date-sensitive embedded chips could stop working properly when the date rolls past December 31, 1999. Embedded business systems control traffic lights, air traffic control, security systems, time clocks, and hospital operating systems, etc. Since the embedded systems run in the background, one has to replace processors and circuit boards for them to function properly.

Cost

The Year 2000 problem is not trivial and its solution is estimated to cost billions of dollars according to Capers Jones (1996), software measurement specialist and CEO of Software Productivity Research, Inc. (SPR). Jones provides estimation of the US costs for finding and fixing the Year 2000 problem. His comments about the seriousness of the Year 2000 problem is supported by other experts such as Dr. Edward Yardeni, Chief Economist and Managing Director of

2

Deutsche Bank Securities. Yardeni, who acquired a reputation by accurately forecasting the long bull market on Wall Street, provides analysis of the economic consequences of the problem and how it could disrupt the US economy (Cairncross, 1998). Media authorities describe Yardeni as the most credible alarmist in the economic arena (Reporting, 1999).

According to a World Bank report, the most frequently cited Y2K repair estimates are the Gartner Group estimates of the cost of a global fix to be up to $600 billion and SPR estimates of a total world-wide fixed cost of $1.6 trillion, including litigation (World, 1998 p16; Feder 1999c; Yourdon & Yourdon, 1999 p554).

Failure to Take Action

Failure to resolve the problem can cause expensive damage that could lead to litigation, possible bankruptcy, and possible business failure. Because of the unique, unfamiliar nature of the Year 2000 problem, no one is able to fully anticipate all of the risks (Yourdon & Yourdon, 1999 p9). In addition to risks, there are several barriers to the Y2K problem such as time, awareness and commitment, information sharing, skills, and other demands on staff. So, the need to plan and implement risk management approaches has become an important priority in preparing for the Year 2000.

While some enterprises are striving to solve the problem, others have resorted to litigation against technology enterprises. As a result of current litigation as well as predictions by the Giga Information Group (Jinnett, Jul 1997), the Gartner Group (Radosevich, 1998) and Jones, law firms are preparing for Y2K legal cases. They are training solicitors to become Y2K savvy, asking questions about when enterprises knew about the two-digit date problem, and monitoring legislative activities to see if governments will introduce new legislation to cap Y2K liabilities.

Research Methodology

In early 1999, SITDRAC commissioned a study to investigate the emergence of the Year 2000 problem as a critical issue for businesses, particularly in the US and Singapore. The Committee requested a chronological list of the events and approaches used by government and legal communities in responding to the problem. The project team identified three questions that drove the analytical requirements of the study.

Research Questions

• What events prompted the recognition of the Y2K problem as a critical issue for governments and businesses, particularly, in Singapore and the US?
• Currently, how are they responding? From legal and legislative perspectives, what approaches have emerged?
• What obstacles and legal cases have emerged and how are they being resolved?

This study provides a chronology of international Y2K events and uses information from the United States (US), United Kingdom (UK), Australia, and Singapore for analysis of the Y2K problem area. In order to customize and update the chronology, it is available in Excel format upon request.

Goals of the Study

• Identify events associated with resolution of the Year 2000 problem & create a chronology.
• Analyze the business, legislative, and legal responses.
• Identify Y2K legislation.
• Outline the legal obstacles and cases that have emerged.

Key Activities Performed

- Searched for Y2K literature reviews and information about the Y2K problem. For example, searched 22 Dialog commercial business databases to identify Year 2000-related publications. Also, searched LEXIS-NEXIS database. The searches used a variety of terms for the Year 2000 problem such as Y2K, millennium bug, and year 2000 compliance.
- Using a knowledge discovery approach, identified and analyzed Y2K news articles, books, conferences, electronic discussion messages, reports, and other documents.
- Interviewed Y2K officials in Singapore.
- Monitored Y2K seminars, conferences, hearings, and participated in Y2K seminars, online discussion forums and news filtering services. Online discussion forums included the Year 2000 Discussion List (year2000-discuss@year-2000.com) and Practicing Lawyers Institute Y2K Legal Forum (pli-y2klaw@pli.edu).
- Used text mining techniques of retrospective tracing, on-line citation and web link analysis to identify patterns among the data. Web link analysis is the use of quantitative measures to analyze web-based resources (Larsen, 1996; Almind & Ingwersen, 1997; Reid, 1997).
- Using Excel, compiled a chronology of Y2K events (see Appendix A).

Chapter 2:   Emergence of the Y2K Problem

Many publications have been written on the root causes of Y2K problem (Jones, 1998 p19; Kappelman & Cappel, 1996; Yourdon & Yourdon, 1999 p540). The root cause is associated with earlier design constraints when computer storage was limited and expensive. Since no one could predict how long software would last, the use of a two-digit date seemed natural and convenient.

According to Schoen, an early Y2K pioneer and former CEO of a Y2K company founded in 1984, data processing professionals have known about the risk associated with the two-digit dates since the 1970s (Gillin, 1984). There is widespread agreement with this (deJager & Bergeon, 1997; Yardeni (www.yardeni.com); Swaine, 1998; Jones, 1998 p157).

Schoen states that by the early 1980s computer capacity was already adequate and there was no justification for continuing to use the two-digit dates (www.flash.net/~bschoen/). Jones (1998, p23) has a different perspective on computer storage capacity. In his book, *The Year 2000 Software Problem*, he states that it was not until the early 1990s and the advent of optical storage that data storage cost declined drastically. He emphasizes that the early 1990s would have been the best time for addressing the Year 2000 problem. During such period, quite a significant amount of applications with two-digit date fields were in daily use throughout the world (Jones, 1998 p23).

A chronology of Year 2000 problem events is provided in Appendix A. Using Y2K events, this study presents analyses from the perspective of how the Year 2000 problem area developed. During the analysis, several patterns emerged such as different responses to the Y2K problem and generation of new knowledge. Therefore, the development of Y2K problem is characterized by the following:

- A diversity of responses to the problem,
- A variety of knowledge creation processes,
- Increased social interactions and information sharing about the problem, and
- An emerging community of Y2K consultants, vendors and specialists (community development).

Using the above characteristics, the Year 2000 problem area is organized into three periods. They are Period 1 1960-1991, Period 2 1992-1996, and Period 3 1997-August 1999. Figure 1 provides a schematic view of the periods.

Figure 1 - Three Periods in Development of Y2K Problem Area

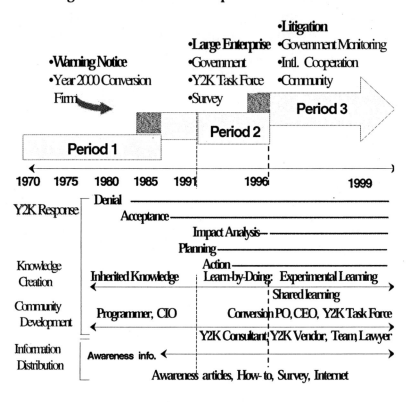

Since the problem area is characterized by a diversity of responses, a Year 2000 response model is used to categorize the responses (Kappelman & Cappel, 1996). For this study, the response model is used to highlight how enterprises reacted to the problem, when they responded and what actions they took. It includes the stages of awareness, denial, anger, acceptance, impact analysis, planning and scheduling, conversion, and testing and implementation.

The response model is available at www.comlinks.com/mag/cirep.htm. According to Kappelman and Cappel, the model uses an analogy of responses that people commonly use to cope with other types of crises such as divorce or terminal illness. It is used extensively in their Year 2000 research.

Using the activities listed in the chronology (Appendix A) and the response model, the following section provides an analysis of how the problem area developed.

Period 1, 1960-1991.   Response - Awareness, Denial, Acceptance

Year 2000 Response

During the first period, 1960-1991, early sightings of the two-digit date problem were identified in the financial and insurance industries.   In the 1970s, enterprises with applications that calculate long-term mortgage and insurance payments started having problems. For example, banks in the US began having problems nearly 30 years ago (Marcoccio, 1998).   In-house manual fixes were used to alleviate the problem.

During this same period, several articles providing early warnings about the two-digit date problem appeared in the technical trade press (Swaine, 1998; Schlesinger &

Derrevere, 1999 p3; Kappelman, 1999). Early warning article about the two-digit date problem was the topic of a Year 2000 Discussion List message dated June 11, 1999 (Kappelman, 1999). In the message, the sender mentioned that there were publications in 1971 and 1979 about the problem. In response to a reply, he provided the following citations to early warning articles:

- Bemer, Bob. What's the Date? *Honeywell Computer Journal*, v.4, 1971.
- Bemer, Bob. *Interface*, 1979.

A follow-up search of the World Wide Web (WWW) and LEXIS-NEXIS identified several articles that mention Bemer's activities in the 1970s. The search queries included Bemer, two-digit date problem and/or date conversion problem. The results are as follows:

- "Bemer wrote an article in *Datamation* back in the 1970s . The article alerted many to the two-digit date problem" (Swaine, 1998).
- "Bemer started warning industry and the government about the forthcoming Y2K problem as early as 1969" (White Paper, nd).
- "Bemer had anticipated what has become known as the Y2K predicament back in 1979" (Septuagenarian, 1998).

According to Schlesinger and Derrevere, there were only four Y2K articles, published between 1982 and 1994, retrieved from the LEXIS-NEXIS commercial database. This research team conducted similar searches using terms such as two-digit date problem, year 2000 problem and date conversion problem. The searches of several commercial databases and the WWW for Year 2000 articles published before 1990, retrieved ten hits. They included articles published in the *Computerworld* as well as two articles published in 1988 in *The New York Times* (Feder, 1988) and *Business Week* (Gelfond, 1988*).* In *Computerworld,* the earliest one was published in 1984 and is entitled "The Problem You May Not Know You Have" (Gillin, 1984). In a follow-up *Computerworld* article on 3 August 1998, the 1984 article is cited as the first article about the Year 2000 problem to appear in a major publication (Gillin, 1998).

In the 1984 article, Schoen was definitive about his prognosis that computers would stop working properly on New Year's Day 2000. He created a Year 2000 software program and started a company (www.flash.net/~bschoen/). However, the idea of a two-digit date problem was met with management resistance because most enterprises were not experiencing date failures. Management did not see the need to invest in a solution. Moreover, the two-digit date problem solution was a new idea that was preventive in nature. Some managers may have felt that the problem (computer failure on Jan 2000) was far too distant in the future.

Feder's 1988 *New York Times* article entitled "For Computers, the Year 2000 May Provide a Bit Traumatic," reported a manager in the Information Resource Management Group at the US Defense Department as saying that very few people were thinking about it. Feder states that:

> "One great comfort for data processing executives is that many of today's problem programs - up to 80 percent by some estimates - will have been replaced by 1999 in the normal course of business. Presumably, new software will be written with the millennium in mind".

Rogers (1995, p216), a diffusion scholar, analyzed the concept of how people accept new ideas of solutions that are preventive in nature. He concluded that people have difficulties in perceiving the relative advantage of adopting a preventive idea because it is a non-event (has not happened yet). Plus, the rewards are not immediate. Furthermore, some people believe that the future problem event will not happen at all (as illustrated in Feder's comments).

Another example of early warning of Year 2000 problem is a 1986 advertisement in *Computing SA* (world-online.net/project2000/north/206.htm). Anderson, a programmer, ran an ad with the headline "Timebomb in Your IBM Mainframe System". The advertisement drew less than a half dozen responses including an admission from a large multinational enterprise that they were aware of the problem and did not anticipate any difficulties in handling it (www.y2ktimebomb.com/Bios/cabio.htm).

Also in the 1980s, some proactive organizations such as the US Social Security Administration (SSA), the Port of Singapore Authority (PSA), and the Treasury Board Secretariat (Canada) recognized that the two-digit date field would become a problem and started to phase in conversion to four-digit dates (Singapore National, 1999; Small, 1998). SSA is the third-largest Federal government software user after the US Defense Department and the Census Bureau (Feder, 1988). A SSA manager said, according to Feder, that those who didn't take the Year 2000 issue seriously were going to be faced with a real problem in the late 1990s.

Comments about Early Warnings

deJager and Bergeon (1997, p220) acknowledged that there were several warnings in the 1980s and early 1990s. But staff in information technology (IT) departments argued that they had no budget and no choices because they weren't calling the shots. deJager and Bergeon believe that there was a failure in communication between the IT staff and management. Management heard and then ignored. Programmers accepted being ignored, opting to remain quiet.

A similar comment is identified in Kappelman and Cappel's (1996) article. Many technical staff were aware of the impending date problem, but CIOs tended to underestimate it. Furthermore, there was limited coverage of the problem in the business press. When their technical managers confronted senior managers with the problem, they may have reacted, If this is such a big problem, why haven't I read anything about it (in the newspapers)?

According to Yourdon and Yourdon (1999, p548), senior business managers generally ignored the date-related problems. Ed Yourdon, editor of *Application Development Strategies* and author, is a widely renowned software methodology authority (deJager & Bergeon, 1997 p ix). Some typical responses include "We'll worry about it next year, when we have more time & budget... I'll let my successor worry about the problem".

As illustrated by these examples, the 1970s and 1980s provided early warnings, lots of denial, procrastination, and limited acceptance by senior management. Some managers doubted the seriousness of the problem because they assumed that an easy technical solution would be provided (Feder, 1988; Nunno, March 1999, p CRS-2; Small, 1998). Others predicted that the problem would escalate.

According to Prochaska, DiClemente, and Norcross (1992), research on how people change addictive behavior such as smoking indicates that many people progress through five stages: pre-contemplation, contemplation, preparation, action, and maintenance. For the Y2K problem, Period 1 is considered as pre-contemplation time because it is the stage that many people had no intention to change their Y2K behavior in the near future. Figure 2 provides an illustration of the changing patterns associated with responding to the Y2K problem.

Figure 2 - Patterns of Change in Responding to Y2K

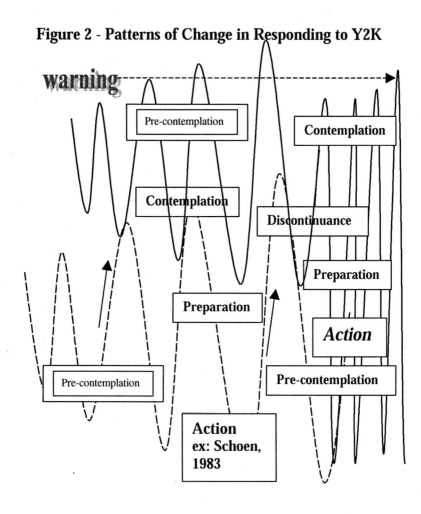

Chapter 3:   Taking Action (Period 2, 1992-1996)

Period 2, 1992-1996. Response - Awareness, Denial, Acceptance, Impact Analysis, Planning

In the second period, there was a substantial increase in Y2K activities.   The activities run parallel to deJager and Bergeon's (1997 p28) suggestions on giving a wake-up call. They recommend several tasks in waking up the world to the seriousness of the date problem.   The tasks include:

- Create awareness,
- Achieve visibility and put a Y2K team in place,
- Conduct an estimate survey to identify IT system failures,
- Establish training programs to get the staff ready to participate in Y2K program,
- Identify cost and policy issues,
- Organize management briefing, and
- Minimize business impact (deJager and Bergeon, 1997).

Most of these tasks were initiated in Period 2.   Figure 3 provides a graphic representation of some events in the second period.

Figure 3 - Y2K Events in Period 2

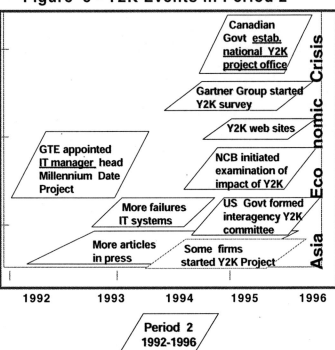

1992 1993 1994 1995 1996

In order to identify when some of the largest US enterprises started their Y2K program, data were collected from enterprises web sites and their Securities and Exchange Commission (SEC) disclosure reports. Using Standard & Poor's (S&P) 500 largest enterprises, 292 enterprises reported the year that they started their Y2K programs. Figure 4 highlights that 62% cited 1996 or 1997 as the year they started their programs. The findings have similarities to results provided by surveys of the progress of the UK's largest 1,000 enterprises towards Year 2000 compliance. In

Figure 4 - S&P Enterprises Y2K Start Date

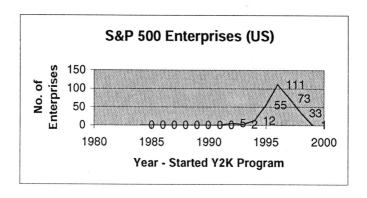

December 1998, a survey was sponsored by Dibb Lupton Alson and Taskforce 2000 (Business, 1999). One of the key findings is that the majority of the top 1,000 UK enterprises initiated work on Year 2000 compliance in 1996 or 1997 (Business, 1999). In 1998, 24% began their compliance activities.

Year 2000 Response

More enterprises experienced IT failures that were associated with two-digit dates. A 1995 ADPAC survey found that 44% of respondents reported that they were already encountering Year 2000 date-related problems in their mainframe applications (Kappelman & Cappel, 1996). Conducting surveys to gather Year 2000 status information was becoming a common activity.

As a result of experiencing date-related problems, several large enterprises such as GTE, Unum Life, Bank of Boston, Chase Manhattan, Kaiser Permanente, and Pacific Union started their millennium conversion projects (Kappelman & Cappel 1996; deJager & Bergeon, 1997 p xii; Jones, 1998; Cohen, 1997 p230). For example in late 1993, GTE Corporation became concerned with date-related problems in some of its applications (deJager & Bergeon, 1997). In response, the enterprise appointed two senior level managers to be in charge of their Millennium Date Conversion Project. Later, GTE (1999) took legal action against the enterprise's five insurance companies to try and get reimbursed for the $400 million spent in Y2K remediation.

In January 1995, an application that calculated five-year payments in the city of Phoenix, Arizona crashed because of two-digit date problems (deJager & Bergeon, 1997, p x). The crash was considered a blessing because the city would have calculated inaccurate payment schedules with potentially disastrous results. Viasoft, a consultant company, was hired to tackle the date problem with a cost estimate of $63 million (deJager & Bergeon, 1997). It is an example of a little-known enterprise that became an overnight Wall Street sensation when the Gartner Group began warning that hundreds of billions of dollars would be spent on Year 2000 work (Feder, 1999a). According to Feder, Viasoft's remediation approach focused on the use of locating and changing dates in the systems codes but that did not prove to be as popular as the windowing approach. The windowing approach involves inserting programming logic to window the dates so as to allow the program to interpret the century as 19 or 20 based on parameters defined by the programmer (deJager & Bergeon, 1999 p76).

Attributes of Early Adopters

Enterprises such as the city of Phoenix, Unum Life, and GTE had several items in common: a large number of customized applications written in different languages, in-house IT departments, substantial IT budgets, and resources for hiring consultants. In order to resolve the Y2K problem, they appointed project leaders, organized project teams, and started planning their Year 2000 strategies. Jones (1998, p8) described them as early and proactive Year 2000 repair groups. In this study, they are classified as early adopters who used the learning-from-doing process to acquire knowledge on how to fix the Year 2000 problem.

The attributes of the early adopters and their Y2k events are listed in Appendix B. They have several similarities to the characteristics identified in the Gartner Group's findings (Marcoccio, 1998 p3). According to the findings, the large enterprises are farthest ahead because they started earlier. Since they were experiencing system failures, they secured larger IT operating budgets that were allocated to fixing the Y2K problem. Furthermore, a large percentage of their IT systems were built in-house so there was less reliance on vendors. Typically, small companies would have purchased a much larger percentage of IT systems from vendors and have less cash reserves and other resources to fix their Y2K problem. Small enterprises needed to wait for vendor solutions.

Figure 5 provides a summary of early adopters' attributes. For organization diffusion, the attributes of early adopters of Y2K support Rogers' (1995 p379) hypothesis that early adopters are large organizations that are highly respected, have more resources including technical expertise, and are willing to decrease uncertainty about a new idea by testing it.

Also during this period, some governments became active in investigating the Y2K problem and establishing an interagency committee or task force. Appendix C lists government activities associated with the problem. For example, in 1995, the National Computer Board (NCB), Singapore, started to examine the potential impact of the millennium bug on Singapore. At about the same time, the US Office of Management Budget (OMB) established an interagency Y2K committee, led by the Social Security Administration (SSA), to initiate awareness among Federal agencies. Since SSA had started to address its date problem, it had experience in the identification and assessment of the Y2K problem. These events and the relevant references (including web addresses) are listed in Appendix C and the chronology.

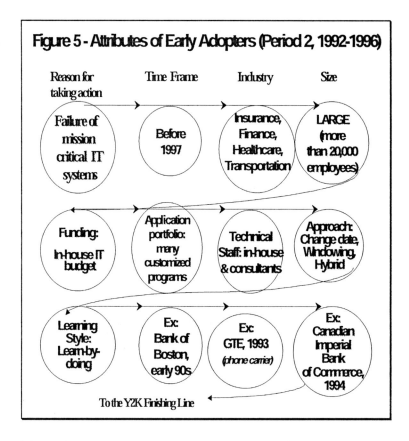

Figure 5 - Attributes of Early Adopters (Period 2, 1992-1996)

Reason for taking action	Time Frame	Industry	Size
Failure of mission critical IT systems	Before 1997	Insurance, Finance, Healthcare, Transportation	LARGE (more than 20,000 employees)
Funding: In-house IT budget	Application portfolio: many customized programs	Technical Staff: in-house & consultants	Approach: Change date, Windowing, Hybrid
Learning Style: Learn-by-doing	Ex: Bank of Boston, early 90s	Ex: GTE, 1993 (phone carrier)	Ex: Canadian Imperial Bank of Commerce, 1994

To the Y2K Finishing Line

The US government's interagency committee developed a web site (www.itpolicy.gov/mks/yr2000) to share information and issued a best practice report. The report includes a comprehensive conversion plan and provides a method for dividing Y2K conversion activities into five phases: awareness, assessment, renovation, validation, and implementation. The five phases were adopted by federal agencies. Also, many private enterprises and national governments have adopted the phased approach (Nunno, 1999 p CRS-4). An analysis of S&P 500 enterprises' Y2K web sites and SEC corporate disclosure reports indicated that 320 (64%) enterprises reported using the phased approach.

In addition, a World Bank (1998 p54) report recommends the use of the interagency committee's resources and the 5 phases project management approach to implement national Y2K projects. For each phase, it outlines the objectives, tasks and associated processes as they relate to the Y2K project life cycle. Furthermore, the report provides an overview of the application of the triage strategy to the Y2K problem. The triage strategy recognizes that all repairs can not be made before the January 1st deadline date. It means that one must consider and treat first the most critical systems and applications, most at risk and with high probability to survive; to waste no resource if there is no concrete possibility of success; and to be realistic (World, 1998; Yourdon & Yourdon, 1999 p566). For an example of the triage strategy, Yourdon and Yourdon recommend deJager's, a Y2K guru, illustration using the airline industry.

In 1996, the House Government Reform and Oversight Committee started hearings to investigate the problem (Nunno, 1999 p CRS-8). In addition, the Congressional Research Service (CRS) provided a study of the federal government's Year 2000 problem (Jinnett, 1997). Also, the United Kingdom (UK) had parliamentary hearings (Jones, 1997 p157; Science, 1998). A summary of government responses is included in the next chapter.

According to Jones (1998 p60), 1996 was a significant year because the problem became a major business issue for management. The problem posed serious business and personal liability threats to executives. Since networked computer systems are the backbone for many businesses and government operations, failure to solve the Year 2000 problem may cause expensive damages that could lead to lawsuits and even loss of lives (Jones, 1998).

Now that the problem is being publicized and technical solutions are available, an effective defense against Year

2000 damage suits may be difficult. Jones predicts that the consequences of not solving the year 2000 problem are more hazardous to executives than the costs of solving them. He recommends that executives use a strategy of due diligence and thoroughness in resolving the Year 2000 problem.

Jones' Predictions Regarding Litigation

Jones (1996; 1998, p153) outlined six kinds of Year 2000 litigation that may occur. They are:

- Litigation filed by clients whose products, finances, or investments have been damaged,
- Litigation filed by shareholders of companies whose software does not safely make the year 2000 transition,
- Litigation associated with any deaths or injuries derived from the year 2000 problem,
- Class-action litigation filed by various affected customers of computers or software packages,
- Litigation filed by companies that used solutions from outsourcers, vendors, contractors, consultants, or commercial year 2000 tools, where the Year 2000 problems still slipped through and caused damage, and
- Litigation against hardware manufacturers such as computer companies and defense contractors if the year 2000 problem resides in hardware or embedded microcode as well as software (Jones, 1996; 1998).

Chapter 4: Knowledge Creation and Sharing of Y2K Information (Period 2)

Knowledge Creation *(Period 2, 1992-1996.)*

Since there were no manuals or documentations on how to resolve the Y2K problem, the early adopters' organizational learning processes will provide data for researchers interested in knowledge creation of this global problem. The research by Huber (1991) and Nonaka (1994) on organizational learning provide useful models for analyzing Y2K knowledge creation, information sharing, information interpretation, and information marketing.

Without the early adopters pioneering organizational learning processes for resolving the Y2K problem, the Y2K problem would have been more difficult to accept. At least, there were champions acquiring real experience in resolving the problem. Later, they would play a major role in sharing their experiences at Y2K conferences, seminars and Congressional hearings. In addition, some experiences became best practice cases for the Society of Information Management (SIM) Year 2000 Working Group (www.year2000.unt.edu). The Group was formed in 1996 and conducted a longitudinal study of Year 2000 progress (Kappelman & Keeling, 1997 p264).

Also during this period, more articles were published in the trade and popular press that describe the potential impact of problem. Figure 6 provides summary results of the searches of 22 Dialog commercial business databases to identify Year 2000 problem publications. The searches included a variety of terms such as year 2000 computer problem, millennium bug, millennium time bomb, date conversion problem, Y2K, and year 2000 compliance.

Figure 6 - Results of Searching 22 Business Databases via DIALOG (Feb,99)

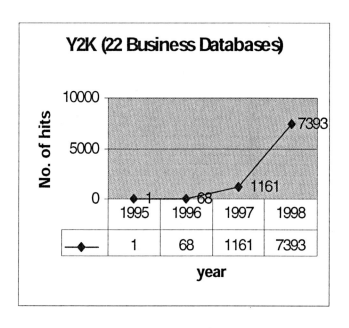

Y2K (22 Business Databases)

	1995	1996	1997	1998
◆	1	68	1161	7393

year

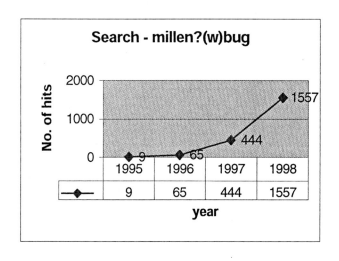

Search - millen?(w)bug

	1995	1996	1997	1998
◆	9	65	444	1557

year

According to the results, there was a substantial increase in publications in 1997.

Examples of publications during the 2nd period are deJager's (1993) classic Doomsday article and articles published in *Datamation*. Feder (1998) described the Doomsday article as the information-age alarm that stirred the information systems (IS) industry into taking the Year 2000 problem seriously. Some government and court officials agree with this (Kenney & Gerwinat, 1999 p4).

In an interview with deJager, Feder labels him as the "Paul Revere for the Year 2000 computer crisis". deJager has become a folk hero in his crusade to publicize the problem. He averages more than five interviews a day. He has given presentations at Y2K conferences and to the world's central bankers in Basel, Switzerland, US Congressional hearings, chief executives at the World Economic Forum in Davos, Switzerland, and Y2K national experts in the UK. In addition, deJager has authored articles and books on Y2K (deJager & Bergeon 1997; 1999; deJager 1993). Diffusion scholars will label deJager as a change agent. A change agent is an individual or organization that influences people to adopt the new idea (Rogers, 1995 p339).

In 1995, deJager created a Year 2000 web site (www.year2000.com). Feder, Yourdon and Yourdon, and Jones describe the web site as a focal point of news and discussion about the problem. According to Yourdon and Yourdon (1999, p608), deJager created the first serious web site for Y2K. It continues to be one of the most heavily visited Y2K sites. Yourdon and his daughter visit the press clippings section of the site almost daily because it covers U.S., Canadian, British, and Australian media (Yourdon & Yourdon 1999, p608).

To assess the popularity and influence of the web site, a web linkage search was conducted to identify how many external web pages are linked to deJager's site. Jackson (1999) describes the process of deciding to create an external hypertext link to someone's web site as a strategic decision. Reid and Bauer (1999) describe it as a process in which someone has to:

- Identify and assess the web site.
- Decide why it is important to link to the site.
- Create a comment as to why the web site is being recommended to others.
- Capture the web address and contact the site to advise them that you want to link to their home page.
- Give web address to web master so that he/she can set up the hypertext link.

In December 1998, 345 web pages linked to deJager's site while in August 1999, 1300 web pages were found to have linked to his web site. deJager's site can be viewed as a mechanism for information exchange between change agents and other interested persons including the media. A network analysis of the site will identify how it is a reference point in Y2K social systems involving many other actors and how it influences the spread of information about the Y2K problem. For example, the following Table identifies organizations that have hypertext links to deJager's web site:

Table – Web Pages that Link to deJager's Web Site (www.year2000.com)

Organization	Role	Immediate Audience	Web Address (URL)
Accounting for the Year 2000 (Y2K) Problem	Subject Directory to Y2K information for Accountant	Accountant	www.bus.or st.edu/facult y/brownc/Y ear2000/Yea r2000.htm
Legal Services Corporation (LSC) Office	Extranet site for Legal Organization (US Govt.)	Legal Community	www.rin.lsc. gov/rinboard /technology/ y2000.htm
SBA: Year 2000 Issues Affecting Small Business Hotlist	US Small Business Administration (SBA), (US Govt.)	Small Business Community	www.sbaonl ine.sba.gov/ hotlist/year2 000.html
State Department	Overseas Travel Information (US Govt.)	Travelers - Overseas	travel.state.g ov/y2kca.ht ml
Y2K Gateway CIO Council Committee	Interagency committee (US Govt.)	Government Agencies (US)	www.itpolic y.gsa.gov/m ks/yr2000/y 2karts.htm

How-to Information

In addition to the early awareness resources such as deJager's web site, some resources provided detailed how-to

28

information. Kappelman and Cappel (1996), in their study of how to facilitate an effective response, provided instructions on how to take action to remediate the problem. In particular, they identified how Chief Information Officers (CIOs) should stress to top management that the Year 2000 problem is not just a technical but also an organizational problem. Since it involves the failure of business systems that are not compliant, it can cause the failure of entire business operations. Later, the article appeared at Alan Simpson (Comlinks web site www.comlinks.com) and in the *Year 2000 Problem: Strategies and Solutions from the Fortune 100* (Kappelman & Cappel, 1997 p58). Y2K information was being disseminated and packaged into different forms.

How-to information provides instruction on how to use a new idea, properly. Rogers (1995, p165) considers it important in the diffusion of a new idea because it helps to reduce complexity and makes the idea easier to accept. For example, Jones' (1996) 80-page report on quantifying software maintenance cost for Y2K repairs is readily available to the public via his enterprise's web site (www.spr.com/library).

Using software demographics data from different sources, the report provides several methods for estimating software maintenance cost and manpower requirements as well as how to deal with risks of business failure and litigation. Excerpts from the report have been integrated into other publications such as Jones (1997 p12), Rubin, World Bank (1998 p65) report, and others (Jones, 1998 p xvii).

Although they are not available to the general public, other sources of quantitative Y2K data are available from consultancy services such as the Gartner Group, the Meta Group, and the Giga Group (Jones, 1998 p xviii). Also, the SIM Working Group collected cost data from 173

29

respondents for its Year 2000 survey (Kappelman, Fent & Prybutok, 1997 p279).

A highly cited service that started during this period is the Gartner Group's worldwide survey of enterprises' and governments' Year 2000 readiness -- packaged as a quarterly fee-based report series (Feder, 1999c). The service provides an understanding of the total risk of the Year 2000 problem by collecting data on an enterprise's Year 2000 status, methods, plans, and costs (gartner5.gartnerweb.com/public/static/home/00073955.html). The related survey in the report involved more than 15,000 enterprises from 87 countries (Year 2000, 28 Oct 1998). The data were gathered through interviews, client inquiry meetings, and self-assessment surveys of enterprises, government agencies, legal firms, vendors, etc. Some important contributions of the service are as follows:

- It helped to increase awareness of the global Year 2000 problem and its complexity.
- It pioneered methodologies for measuring an enterprise's Y2K compliance status and predicting Year 2000 related failures, e.g. the COMpliance Progress And Readiness (COMPARE Ratings) and the COMPARE Operational Risk Evaluation (CORE).
- It provided managers and government leaders with estimates of the size, global readiness levels, and potential impact of the Y2K problem (Year 2000, 28 Oct 1998).

Feder's (1999c) article of the Gartner Group's early entrance to Y2K area presents the pros and cons of the Gartner Group's ratings. According to Feder, the Gartner Group's popularity in the Year 2000 problem area rose rapidly after a 1996 congressional hearing when it was estimated that US enterprises might spend as much as $600 billion dealing with the century date problem. Today, its ratings and data permeate Year 2000 mass media articles, books, and CEO boardrooms.

A critic of the publicity often given to the Gartner Group's estimates include Bruce McConnell, head of the World Bank's recently formed International Y2K Cooperation Center (Feder, 1999c). "McConnell says that as a Y2K coordinator in a foreign country, you need to know what Gartner is saying about you" (Feder, 1999c).

Yourdon and Yourdon (1999, p554) describe the widely publicized estimates of the Gartner Group as crude approximations. According to them, 1996-1997 was the time that several consulting and research organizations began sizing the Year 2000 problem. In addition, they compared estimates prepared by the Gartner Group, Rubin, Yardeni, and Jones. Of these, Jones' is described as having the most detailed figures, and the ones that appear to be most widely accepted by other professionals and researchers in the field (Yourdon & Yourdon, 1999 p554).

Although Yourdon and Yourdon criticize the Gartner Group's widely publicized ratings, the estimates are cited in their book such as the 1998 Gartner Group's estimates on embedded systems (p412), the status of Japan's Y2K awareness (p494), and an estimate of Y2K impact on banking (p175).

Information Sharing (Period 2, 1992-1996.)

In addition to the Garner Group's fee-based service, other Y2K resources became available including government reports, newsletters, and news articles. As mentioned earlier, new web sites devoted to the Y2K issue, such as deJager's Year 2000 Information Center (www.year2000.com) and

Yardeni's (www.yardeni.com), were set up. Internet services such as web sites, email, and discussion forums provided a means of sharing information, distributing Y2K surveys and newsletters to keep current on latest developments, and identifying whether a product was Y2K compliant. In fact, a vendor compliance form was the major mechanism for collecting readiness information and determining supply chain risks (Marcoccio, 1998 p3). However, as it turned out vendor compliance statements went through dynamic and frequent revisions. To track such frequent revisions, some enterprises resorted to the use of in-house compliance databases and/or subscribed to commercial compliance tracking services. One example is the Infolaint Company that has reported roughly 3,300 Y2K compliance status changes since they began tracking this data in 1997 (www.infoliant.com). Later, more enterprises moved from compliance statements and surveys only for data gathering purposes, to requesting face-to-face direct interviews.

Another means of information sharing is a newsletter such as 'Tick, Tick, Tick' (deJager, 1993). The purpose of this newsletter is to bring together people in the IS industry who are concerned with the Year 2000 problem. Other examples include the Information Technology Association of America (ITAA) web site and newsletter (Cohen, 1997 p230). In July 1996, ITAA started reporting on the status of enterprises' Year 2000 projects in a weekly Internet-based newsletter called Year 2000 Outlook. In addition to reporting the latest news and events shaping the Year 2000 problem, Outlook provided stories of specific enterprise activities. Stories were shared by early adopters such as Chubb Group of Insurance Companies, Bank of Boston, Bank of Hawaii, and Union Pacific (Cohen, 1997 p230; deJager & Bergeon, 1997 p xii;. McKendrick, 1997 p252). Also, ITAA awarded its first Year 2000 Certification in 1996 (deJager & Bergeon, 1997; McKendrick).

Also during the second period, enterprises, associations and governments started to organize Year 2000 seminars, talks, and conferences such as SPG Conference, April 1996 (www.spgnet.com) and the DCI's Year 2000 Summit (www.deci.com/y2k). The Year 2000 SPG Conference provided a mechanism for increasing awareness, collaborating, exchanging ideas, networking, and information sharing. In addition, it provided a platform for the introduction and demonstration of Year 2000 vendor products.

The Internet provided an electronic mechanism to support social networking. It supported the dissemination, display, marketing, and discussion of conference papers, product releases, conference announcements, speakers' biographic data, and conference proceedings. In addition, some web sites such as Year 2000 Information Center provided electronic archives for retrieving Y2K full-text conference papers, reports, articles, book chapters, fee-based discussion forum, as well as reviewing Year 2000 tools. This Information Center evolved into a web portal frequented by journalists who are covering the Y2K scene (www.facsnet.org).

Furthermore, a community of outspoken Y2K inquisitors started to evolve such as Dr. Gary North, a historian. He is an outspoken critic of the Year 2000 problem and has a web site, created in September 1996, that has become one of the prominent sources of materials on Y2K (www.garynorth.com). According to Yourdon and Yourdon (1999, p609), North's web site covers a much broader area than YahooY2K and deJager's web sites. As of October 1998, North had accumulated nearly 3,000 articles, grouped into categories (Yourdon & Yourdon). He provides a direct link to the documents on the Internet, as well as his summary and interpretation of the significance of Y2K events. For example, he provides an analysis of Schoen's attempt to start a Y2K business in 1984.

Emerging Community of Y2K Consultants and Companies (*Period 2, 1992-1996.*)

The creation, marketing, and utilization of Year 2000 tools became major tasks for the emergingYear 2000 repair industry. According to Jones (1998 p175; 1997b p206), the Y2K repair industry started roughly in January 1995. Jones (p175) says the industry can be viewed from three broad categories:

- Companies that sell Y2K assistance and repair tools for various languages,
- Companies that sell Y2K advice and programming assistance (outsourcing), and
- Companies that sell both programming assistance and tools.

deJager and Bergeon (1997, p151) predicted that the inventory of Y2K tools will exceed 3,000. They examine the different types of tools relevant to the millennium update project, benefits to be derived from implementing such tools, and selection implications. In addition, they focus on developments in the outsourcing industry in Y2K problem area. They describe the pros and cons of in-house and outsourced Y2K remediation strategies.

The emerging repair industry was stimulated by the early adopters. For many of the early Year 2000 conversion projects, the teams compiled inventories of Year 2000 tool requirements, purchased or created Year 2000 tools, and hired consultants. Appendix B highlights some of the approaches of the early adopters. For example, Healthsource-Provident Administrators Inc., a health insurance enterprise, started its Year 2000 program in 1995 (Kucera, 1997 p257).

Without resolution of their date-related problems, Healthsource-Provident faced business failure. Because of time constraints, limited budget and conflicting agenda, the enterprise decided to use a hybrid approach (combination of date expansion & data windowing) but could not find the appropriate tools. So they created their own tool, a smart bridging approach. The technique combined file expansion solution with the flexibility of a hybrid approach and the speed of data-windowing techniques (Kucera, 1997). The new technology was used to form a new company called Bridging Data Technology, Inc. (www.bridging.com).

With increased awareness of the complexity and interrelated dimensions of the Year 2000 problem, practical experiences in trying to resolve the problem such as the experience of Healthsource-Provident, and emerging repair industry, the Year 2000 problem has progressed from a purely technical problem to a major business issue on management's agenda. The problem has been diffused beyond the technical community to senior management's boardrooms.

Chapter 5:   Further Development of Y2K Remediation Responses

Period 3, 1997 - 1999 (August). Response - Awareness, Denial, Acceptance, Planning, Conversion, Testing, Contingency Planning, Implementation, & Litigation

In the third period, there were more activities devoted to problem resolution, substantial increase in government and international participation, increased number of Y2K publications, increased specializations and emergence of a community of Y2K specialists, and a high amount of social interaction such as sharing of information and attendance at Y2K conferences. According to British Telecom's Chief Millennium Bug Coordinator, the Y2K issue is requiring enterprises to cooperate and collaborate with competitors - so that others can profit from ground-breaking efforts (Craig, 1997). The Y2K problem area is maturing. Figure 7 provides a graphic presentation of events in the third period.

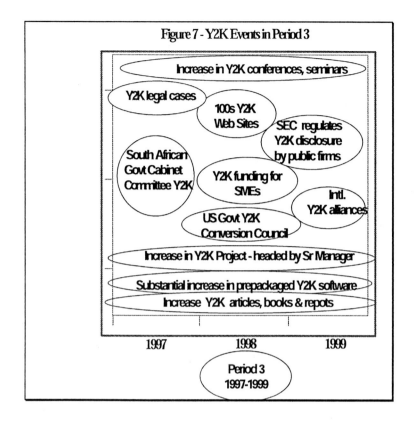

Figure 7 - Y2K Events in Period 3

Increase in Y2K conferences, seminars

Y2K legal cases

100s Y2K Web Sites

SEC regulates Y2K disclosure by public firms

South African Govt Cabinet Committee Y2K

Y2K funding for SMEs

Intl. Y2K alliances

US Govt Y2K Conversion Council

Increase in Y2K Project - headed by Sr Manager

Substantial increase in prepackaged Y2K software

Increase Y2K articles, books & repots

1997   1998   1999

Period 3
1997-1999

Year 2000 Response

During this period, several common themes ran through
much of the Y2K literature. Firstly, larger enterprises are
generally better prepared for the problem than small
organizations (Miller & Stoddart, 1999 p19; Marcoccio,
1998). Secondly, more governments have become active in
helping to resolve and increase awareness of the problem.
Thirdly, some regional variations in the state of Y2K
preparedness have been identified (Miller & Stoddart, 1999
p19; Marcoccio, 1998). This section addresses the themes.

Managers at large, medium, and small size enterprises were
becoming aware of the seriousness of the Year 2000 problem

37

through increased coverage in the popular and business press as well as Y2K presentations at management conferences. According to the Gartner Group, large enterprises are generally furthest ahead in their Y2K preparations (Marcoccio, 1998; Miller & Stoddart, 1999 p19).

Additionally, the professional and trade associations were becoming active in increasing awareness and surveying its members on their Y2K status. Some managers were beginning to ask questions and seek information on the potential impacts to their business operations. The oil industry provides an excellent example. According to Miller and Stoddart (1999 p34), the American Petroleum Institute (API), the National Gas Council (NGC), and the UK Offshore Operators Association (UKOOA), have made major efforts to enhance their members' Y2K awareness. The *World Oil* magazine and the *Oil and Gas Journal* have reviewed the state of the oil industry's Y2K readiness. Some services have commented that the literature on Y2K readiness, in general and particularly in the oil industry, is too narrowly-focused on North American operations. There seems to be a relative lack of information on other regions such as the Middle East or South America that are important in the oil supply chain (Miller & Stoddart, 1999).

The aforementioned Y2K activities resulted in large, medium, and small size organizations initiating Year 2000 programs. Large enterprises, like the Lockheed Martin Corporation (www.lmco.com/minn/year2000.htm), Alcan Aluminum (www.alcan.com), America Online (www.aol.com), Shell, and Nike Inc., started their Year 2000 programs in 1997. Most used a phased approach for organizing their compliance efforts.

For instance in May 1997, a company-wide project was established to identify and resolve the Y2K issues in Nike. The project basically covers categories of IT systems, non-IT systems such as climate control and security systems, and partners such as suppliers and customers (www.nikebiz.com/y2k/discos.shtml). Nike has organized its effort around the six-phased approach.

For Nike, the phases include:

+ Inventory systems,
+ Assessment of risks and impact,
+ Prioritize projects,
+ Fix, replace or develop contingency plans for non-compliant systems,
+ Test and on-going quality control, and
+ Audit results (www.nikebiz.com/y2k/discos.shtml).

Independent consultants were hired to analyze and develop testing and quality assurance standards as well as contingency plans. For its business partners, Nike is trying to assess the compliance of its major suppliers and customers. Surveys and formal communication are used to determine the level of readiness and potential impact on Nike's business operations.

Although more enterprises initiated their Y2K preparations during this period, studies indicate that small enterprises are still plagued with procrastination. According to Yourdon and Yourdon (1999 p xxii), recent surveys indicate that approximately 75% of small businesses around the world have not yet begun working on Y2K. In the US, surveys indicate that approximately 40% of the small companies don't plan to spend any time or money on the problem (Yourdon & Yourdon, 1999).

To further explain why more enterprises started their Y2K programs during this period, let's focus on some expert opinion and government activities. Marcoccio (1998), leader of Y2K research at the Gartner Group, provided expert testimony to the US Senate Special Committee on the Year 2000 Problem on 7 October 1998. He identified several reasons why more companies began to address the Year 2000 Problem:

- A failure occurred affecting a mission critical business process,
- Regulatory mandate and possible penalties,
- Fear of internal litigation due to lack of due diligence, and
- Customer pressures (Marcoccio, 1998).

Government Response *(Period 3, 1997 - 1999, August.)*

Governments of such countries as the US, Singapore, Australia, Canada, United Kingdom (UK), and South Africa became more actively involved in the resolution of the Y2K problem. Many of these governments responded to the Y2K problem by investigating the problem, organizing, coordinating & monitoring national Y2K activities, providing funding, increasing awareness in private and public sectors, and analyzing issues deserving Y2K legislation. Appendix C outlines major responses of several governments and enacted legislations. They are summarized in Figure 8. The following section will focus only on some of the major responses by the US and Singapore governments.

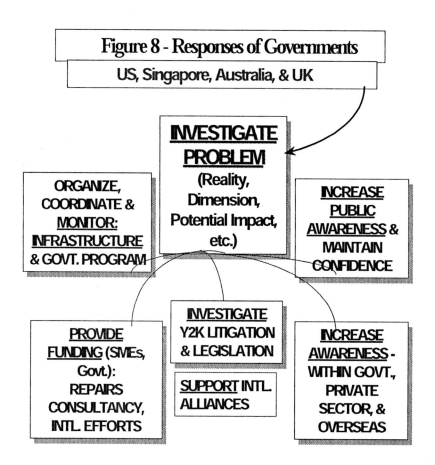

Figure 8 - Responses of Governments
US, Singapore, Australia, & UK

INVESTIGATE PROBLEM
(Reality, Dimension, Potential Impact, etc.)

ORGANIZE, COORDINATE & MONITOR: INFRASTRUCTURE & GOVT. PROGRAM

INCREASE PUBLIC AWARENESS & MAINTAIN CONFIDENCE

PROVIDE FUNDING (SMEs, Govt.): REPAIRS CONSULTANCY, INTL. EFFORTS

INVESTIGATE Y2K LITIGATION & LEGISLATION

SUPPORT INTL. ALLIANCES

INCREASE AWARENESS - WITHIN GOVT., PRIVATE SECTOR, & OVERSEAS

US Government *(Period 3, 1997 - 1999, August).*

During this period, more government officials became convinced of the seriousness of the Y2K problem. Generally, governments have been slower than private enterprises to assess their Y2K problems and take action (Small, 1998). In the US, Congress working through several Congressional committees, led the American government into an understanding of the Y2K problem.

Using the Congressional hearings, Congressmen such as Senators Moynihan and Bennett were able to gather empirical data to convince top government officials of the economic importance of taking concerted action to resolve the Y2K problems. The full-text Congressional Research Service (CRS) report on Congressional issues and approaches to resolving the Y2K problem provides a detailed outline of events (Nunno, 1999). The report is available in Appendix D.

In many Congressional hearings, expert witnesses such as deJager (1996), Jinnett (Jul 1997), Marcoccio (1998), and Yardeni (1997, 1998a) testified on the importance and potential legal consequences of Y2K problems in one of the world's most wired governments. Jinnett's testimony focused on assessing:

- The magnitude of the Year 2000 computer problem and its impact on the financial services industry and U.S. consumers,
- Business risks associated with the Year 2000 computer problem,
- Adequacy of risk management and remediation efforts being undertaken, and
- Possible government roles and regulations in connection with the remediation process.

He stated that

> "The initial Gartner Group estimate that the total cost of correcting the Y2K problem worldwide would total $300 to $600 billion was originally thought excessive by some. For example, J.P. Morgan conducted an independent analysis and estimated the total corrective cost for the Y2K problem worldwide to be in the range of $200 billion. Recently, however, J. P. Morgan reevaluated their $200 billion estimate and advised that the Gartner Group estimate might not be as "outrageously high" as originally thought. Recent announcements by various entities of their individual estimated Y2K corrective costs (e.g., Chase Manhattan Bank at approximately $250 million) indicate that Y2K corrective work will indeed be costly" (Jinnett, Jul 1997).

Congress commissioned the General Accounting Office (GAO), the investigative arm of Congress, to conduct surveys of Y2K readiness and its impact on the Federal government. Furthermore, several specialists provided recommendations on how the US government should confront the millennium bug problem (Jinnett, Jun 1997; Johnson, Rosmond & Kappelman, 1997 p225; Marcoccio, 1998).

Financial Sector

The US Senate Banking, Housing and Urban Affairs Committee, and the Subcommittee on Financial Services and Technology found that the hearing process provided an avenue for coordination and monitoring of the financial sector. In addition, the results of the hearings were used to justify a recommendation for a national shift to a centralized monitoring and compliance approach to Y2K.

Although the idea of a "Czar" was initially presented by Senator Moynihan in 1996 when he introduced a Senate Bill proposing the creation of a bipartisan National Commission on Y2K, it was not until February 1998 that President Clinton appointed a "Y2K Czar" to chair his newly formed President's Council on Year 2000 Conversion (Nunno, 1999). This move represented a more centralized and coordinated approach for monitoring compliance by government agencies and those responsible for key infrastructures.

The government identified five crucial sectors, namely: finance, utilities, transportation, healthcare, and telecommunications. The US financial sector's initiatives are used here to illustrate the process of centralized coordination and monitoring of key infrastructures. Since institutions in the financial sector frequently deal with date-driven calculations and telecommunication networks, they obviously are heavily impacted by the Year 2000 problem.

As mentioned earlier, some financial institutions had already encountered Year 2000 problems. With the sensitive nature of financial services, major Y2K problems can lead to economic chaos and loss of consumer confidence. Finally, for multinational enterprises doing business in Europe, the need to handle the single European currency (the "euro") was necessary as this may exacerbate the difficulties arising out of the Year 2000 problem.

As a result of early attention to the problem and extensive regulatory and Congressional interventions, the financial sector ranks ahead of virtually all other industries in Y2K remediation (Investigation, 1999 p79; Marcoccio, 1998).

According to a US congressional report, the US financial sector has six regulatory agencies that have made considerable progress in tracking and monitoring compliance among banks, thrift and credit unions (Investigating, 1999 p5). They are:

- Federal Financial Institutions Examination Commission (FFIEC),
- Office of Thrift Supervision (OTS),
- Federal Reserve Board (FRB),
- Securities and Exchange Commission (SEC),
- Federal Deposit Insurance Corporation (FDIC), and
- National Credit Union Association (NCUA).

SEC

The SEC was formed by the US Congress in 1933 to protect investors in the wake of the Great Depression.

Based on a request from Senator Bennett, a member of the U.S. Senate Banking, Housing and Urban Affairs Committee and Chairman of the Subcommittee on Financial Services and Technology, the remediation work of each regulatory agency was reviewed by the US General Accounting Office (GAO). Some major initiatives in the US regulation and compliance with such regulations for the financial sector are illustrated in Figure 9. They are described in Appendix E.

Because of Congressional criticism regarding the lack of information on the Y2K readiness of publicly listed enterprises, the Subcommittee on Financial Services & Technology put pressure on the Chairman of the SEC to effect such a reporting mechanism. SEC responded to the criticism by saying that they wanted to handle the problem of disclosure on their own initiatives without additional legislation such as the newly introduced Y2K Computer Remediation & Shareholder (CRASH) Protection Act of 1997. In July 1998, SEC approved strict guidelines on the Y2K information that must be disclosed in order to ensure

Figure 9 - US and Singapore Governments Compliance Reporting Frameworks for Financial Sector

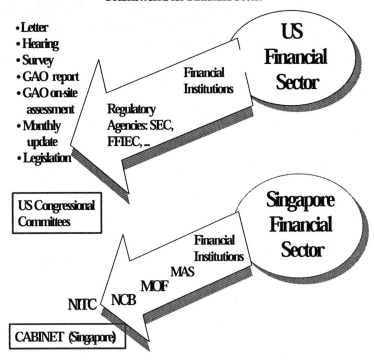

- Letter
- Hearing
- Survey
- GAO report
- GAO on-site assessment
- Monthly update
- Legislation

US Financial Sector

Financial Institutions

Regulatory Agencies: SEC, FFIEC, ...

US Congressional Committees

Singapore Financial Sector

Financial Institutions

MAS
MOF
NITC NCB

CABINET (Singapore)

that investors are not 'left in the dark' regarding problems that may hamper stock prices (Diederich, 1998; Yardeni's Y2K Reporter www.yardeni.com/public/y_19981130.pdf).

According to the SEC, the rules require enterprises to disclose the following information: state of readiness, Y2K costs, Y2K risks, and contingency plans. Enterprises must address the Y2K issues when preparing their quarterly and annual financial reports for SEC filing. As a result of the ruling, quarterly and annual reports of publicly-traded enterprises included more Y2K readiness information. The SEC reports are available at SEC's Internet Edgar database (www.progsys.com/) and the Y2K Disclosure Project maintained by Yardeni (www.yardeni.com/cyber.html).

In addition to informing investors and Congress, the SEC-mandated information has been used as another source of Y2K data for journalists and studies by:

- Yardeni (Dec, 1998),
- Triaxsys Research (Investigating, 1999 p85), and
- International Energy Agency (Miller & Stoddart, 1999 p36).

The Gartner Group survey finds some divergence between the actual status of Y2K compliance and the enterprise's disclosure to the SEC (Miller & Stoddart, 1999 p23). In Yardeni's Y2K Reporter (www.yardeni.com/y2kreporter.html) for November and December 1998, he examined corporate progress by studying Y2K budget data available in some of the third quarter SEC filed reports. Focusing on S&P 500 enterprises, he found that at the top-end of the list are financial sector firms (53.3%) while at the extreme opposite are the utility firms (31.4%).

In Yardeni's series focusing on corporate disclosure statements, he also analyzed how many S&P enterprises were choosing to replace their computer systems with enterprise resource planning (ERP) software sold by System Application Products (SAP) of Germany (www.yardeni.com/public/y_19981214.pdf). ERP is an integrated software package designed to provide complete integration of an enterprise's business information processing systems from accounting and human resources to manufacturing plus integration of all related data (Gelinas, Sutton & Oram, 1999). Although there are other products available such as PeopleSoft and Baan, SAP R/3 is the dominant player with over 80% of the market by most estimates (Gelinas, Sutton & Oram, p5-11).

SAP software is reported to be Y2K compliant from the product's inception five years ago (www.sap-ag.de/y2000/). With the expense associated with ERP, large enterprises such as Goodyear, General Motors, and General Mills have been the predominant implementors of ERP systems. Although Yardeni analyzed 415 enterprises' disclosure statement, very few indicated that they were replacing their systems with SAP. They seem to be opting for remediation (Yardeni, 1998). However, he did identify 18 enterprises such as Reebok, Gillette, and Schumberger that are counting on new SAP systems for Y2K compliance (www.yardeni.com/public/y_19981214.pdf).

Since Yardeni was also concerned about relying on SEC reports for getting Y2K readiness information on large enterprises, he created several new sources for collecting independent Y2K data such as Yardeni's Peoples Poll (www.peoplepolls.com/home.asp#B6) and Y2K Behavior Monitor (www.yardeni.com/cyber.html). Described as the world's first online chart room, the Behavior Monitor tracks 12 indicators such as Eurodollar futures, money market mutual funds, manufacturing inventories, and high-tech orders (www.yardeni.com/public/y2k_c.pdf).

Singapore Government (*Period 3, 1997 - 1999, August*).

Extensive regulatory involvement and initiatives for the financial industries were also evident in other countries' Y2K national readiness activities such as Australia and Singapore. In Singapore, the National Computer Board (NCB) is the government agency appointed to head Y2K remediation efforts as it is the nation's IT authority. Since its major role is to drive government IT conversion and promote national IT awareness, it serves as the secretariat in the national Y2K coordination and monitoring chain.

Singapore's national Y2 coordination and compliance monitoring focuses on government services and key infrastructure sectors such as financial services, utilities, transportation, healthcare, and telecommunications. Similar to several other countries such as the US and Australia, the Y2K remediation tasks are decentralized while the coordination and monitoring are centralized with periodic reports to top government officials.

For example in the financial sector in Singapore, the Monetary Authority of Singapore (MAS) has regulatory responsibilities over more than 500 banks and financial institutions (www.mas.gov.sg). MAS is the statutory board and regulator responsible for raising awareness and facilitating Y2K efforts in the financial sector. It is working with financial regulators overseas as well as Singapore government agencies to address Y2K issues. MAS has adopted guidelines and testing procedures established by the Basle Committee on Banking Supervision's Guidelines (www.mas.gov.sg/y2000/role/close-c.html).

MAS issued several circulars and guidelines to financial institutions, conducted surveys, and performed on-site assessments. Following meetings with several organizations such as the Institute of Certified Public Accountants of Singapore (ICPAS), the statutory auditors have also assisted MAS in identifying deficiencies in financial institutions' Y2K remediation programs (www.mas.gov.sg/y2000/role/promotion-c.html).

Working in cooperation with other organizations, MAS and the Stock Exchange of Singapore (SES) require publicly listed enterprises to make a public disclosure of their Y2K readiness (www.mas.gov.sg/y2000/role/disclosure-c.html). Similarly, regulatory authorities in Australia and New Zealand are requiring public disclosure of Y2K readiness for all publicly listed enterprises (Small, 1998).

Since government ministries and key infrastructure enterprises are required to report their progress to the Singapore Cabinet, there are several components in the Y2K monitoring and reporting framework. First, service providers, such as United Overseas Bank (UOB), report their progress to a statutory board. This statutory board summarizes the data and provides a report to the respective government ministry. The government ministry submits the report to NCB which reports to the National Information Technology Committee (NITC). Finally, the NITC forwards its reports and recommendations to the Cabinet.

Figure 9 provides a schematic overview of Singapore and US reporting frameworks in the financial sector. In Singapore, a financial institution such as the Overseas Chinese Banking Corporation (OCBC) reports its Y2K readiness progress to MAS. MAS summarizes the data and provides a report to the Ministry of Finance. The Ministry submits a report to NCB who reports to NITC.

Although the financial sector has major impact on all levels of society, the other major infrastructure sectors including utilities, transportation, healthcare, and telecommunications are equally crucial. All of the major infrastructures are sources of Y2K risks: business systems such as billing, financial, and human resources, operating systems such as substation switching for electric enterprises, reliability and availability issues, and concerns with third party vendors will have to be Y2K compliant (www.wfs.org/y2kcfutil.htm). According to utility experts, there is a high degree of interdependence and complex relations in the utilities industry, with all utilities dependent on both electricity and telecommunications (www.wfs.org/y2kcfutil.htm). Figure 10 provides an illustration of Singapore's Y2K major infrastructure compliance monitoring framework, national awareness and information sharing activities.

As mentioned earlier, many national Y2K task forces or conversion councils are responsible for centralized coordination and monitoring of each sector. The activities and progress of national Y2K programs for different countries can be viewed at several web sites such as Action 2000 (195.92.149.132/report/main.shtml), US State Department (travel.state.gov/y2kca.html), and the World Bank (www.worldbank.org/infodev/y2k/toolkit).

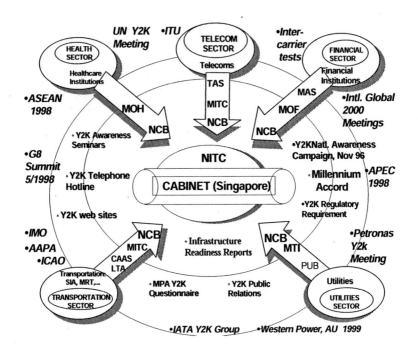

Figure 10 - Illustration of Singapore's Y2K
Infrastructure Compliance

<u>International Response</u> *(Period 3, 1997 - 1999, August).*

Although the concerted effort by the US government seems late in its Y2K readiness, studies indicate that the US is further ahead of other countries in compliance readiness. According to the Gartner Group's survey, the countries that are leading the effort include US, Australia, Canada, UK, Belgium, Denmark, Ireland, Bermuda, and Netherlands (Marcoccio, 1999). Governments have become more active in investigating the national and global threats associated with the problem. According to the survey, the greatest progress has been made by:

- Countries with the highest gross domestic product (GDP),
- Industries heavily focused on financial businesses,
- The enterprises and industries that are the most highly regulated and controlled,
- The largest enterprises, and
- Infrastructure providers in developed countries (Marcoccio, 1999).

Cap Gemini, a major consultancy firm, compiles a "Millennium Index" based on interviews with 1,100 enterprises in eleven OECD countries (Small, 1998). In April 1998, it reported findings broadly comparable with Gartner's, with the US in the lead while France and Germany were trailing behind UK. Other results indicated that 74% of enterprises in Germany would not complete their Year 2000 work on time (Small, 1998).

Sources of information on Y2K readiness in other countries are starting to build up. Two major trends discernible are:

- Small-medium size enterprises (SMEs) are the most at risk, and
- Only a limited number of companies will complete the task before the millennium (Small, 1998).

In respect to the first finding, many surveys indicate that the SMEs are most at risk. In February 1998, Singapore's NCB conducted a survey to assess how prepared SMEs were for the Y2K problem (Chng, 1999). According to an article in the *Economist*, studies conducted in Australia, Korea, and the US provided similar findings (Small, 1998). That is, SMEs plan to take no or inadequate Y2K remediation action.

In Australia, small businesses pose particular concerns (Butt, 1998). In a March 1998 survey, the Australian Bankers Association found that most SMEs had serious misconceptions about the nature and potential impact of Y2K problem (www.bankers.asn.au). Over 40% of SMEs did not plan to take any action as they did not believe they could be impacted. Results seem similar to those from a survey by the Small and Medium Enterprise Agency in Japan (Yourdon & Yourdon, 1999 p497).

In the US, a study commissioned by Wells Fargo and the National Federation of Independent Businesses (NFIB) shows that despite the increasing number of businesses working on the Y2K problem, at least 1.4 million small business owners plan to take no action (Senate Press Release, 1999). Small businesses may have more difficulty addressing potential Y2K problems than larger enterprises because of limited financial and technical resources available.

In response to the need for more funding for SMEs, several countries have arranged for loans or grants such as Singapore's Local Enterprise Computerisation Programme

(LECP), the US Small Business Administration's (SBA) Y2K remediation loans, and UK Action 2000 grant program. In Japan, the Ministry of International Trade and Industry (MITI), in conjunction with the Ministry of Posts and Telecommunications, plan to ask the government for additional such funding for SMEs (Yourdon & Yourdon, 1999 p497).

The second international trend is that only a limited number of countries or companies will complete the task before the millennium. Therefore, risk assessment and contingency plans are essential. Some of the reluctance to move forward on Y2K remediation can be attributed to the Asian Economic Crisis and the Euro conversion.

In such a global economy, the Y2K readiness of neighboring countries is essential for international supply chains. Scott McNealy, chairman of Sun Microsystems, believes that Asia is way behind on its Y2K tasks (Zarocostas, 1999). Also, the Y2K readiness of Japan, a world superpower, is of particular concern for multinational enterprises and the US government. Government reports, news articles, and international surveys highlight the lack of Y2K remediation progress in Japan (Investigating, 1999; Yourdon & Yourdon, 1999 p494; Feder, 1999d).

Research enterprises such as the Gartner Group and the Giga Group say that the European Y2K efforts are competing with other high priorities such as the Euro conversion (Wilson, 1997; Year 2000 in). Many European nations have been focusing their technical efforts on Euro conversion. As previously mentioned, the Euro is the single European currency that was implemented by January 1, 1999 in France, Germany, Italy, Belgium and other countries .

According to the Gartner Group estimates, one-third of all nations won't be ready for the Year 2000 (Yourdon &

Yourdon p499). In 1997, a study by London-based technology consultancy PA Consulting revealed that many IT managers outside of the US worry that their senior executives are still not fully aware of implications of the Y2K problem (Craig, 1997). PA Consulting results appear to support statements by the Gartner Group, who said that 40% of European public-sector systems will be unprepared for Y2K. Cap Gemini's study, in October 1997, found that one in ten UK enterprises will not convert their IT systems in time for the Year 2000 (Craig, 1997).

Joint efforts by governments and private industry associations have shown the most positive results in motivating international progress. Many emerging economies had to find financial resources to fix their year 2000 problems. Financial support came from several international organizations such as the World Bank, UN and APEC (Zarocostas, 1999). These organizations became active in providing funding, increasing awareness, sharing Year 2000 information, assessing their own Year 2000 situation, and sponsoring conferences. At the April 1999 Asia Pacific Economic Cooperation (APEC) Y2K symposium in Singapore, one of the areas of concern was the readiness of SMEs which make up the bulk of the APEC economies (Chng, 1999).

The following are examples of other organizations involved in raising awareness: the Organization for Economic Cooperation and Development (OECD), the Bank for International Settlements (BIS), the European Commission, the Summit of Eight Industrialized Nations, International Airline and Transport Authority (IATA), and International Maritime Organisation (IMO). Some of the organizations are identified in Figure 10 and listed in Nunno's report (Appendix D).

The US and UK contributed millions of dollars to the World Bank's Year 2000 program (Reed, 1999; www.worldbank.org/infodev/y2k/y2kguidelines.htm). With the funding, the World Bank provided Year 2000 repair grants, conference grants, how-to publications, and technical support. For example, Malaysia was allocated $100 million package for their repair efforts and has received technical support from Shell and Singapore's NCB (www.worldbank.org). Argentina was allocated $30 million and $29 million for Sri Lanki (Zarocostas, 1999).

Enterprises in many emerging economies and other SMEs are classified as later adopters of Y2K remediation because they had to wait for economic subsidies and had to respond to external pressures from government authorities, professional associations, and multinational partners. Similar characteristics of late adopters of new ideas have been identified in other studies (Rogers 1995, p269).

For Y2K repairs, the external pressures came from regulatory authorities, legislations, professional associations, international organizations, and partners in the value chain. The pressures can be categorized as coercive, normative, and mimetic processes as described in DiMaggio and Powell's study (1982). These processes often result in enterprises having similar behaviors such as organizing Y2K interdisciplinary teams and using the phased approach to implement Y2K programs (Reid, 1999).

Chapter 6: Knowledge Creation and Sharing of Y2K Information *(Period 3)*

Period 3, 1997 - 1999 (August). Response - Awareness, Denial, Acceptance, Planning, Conversion, Testing, Contingency Planning, Implementation, & Litigation

Knowledge Creation

According to representatives from BP/Amoco, Y2K knowledge has evolved over time (Miller & Stoddart, 1999 p25). But how did the knowledge evolve? Using the case of a multinational enterprise, this section illustrates how a large enterprise is managing its Y2K remediation task and generating new knowledge.

Since the Year 2000 problem is a new, complex and a previously unheard of issue, how did the Shell Group of Companies manage it? Therefore, the case study is approached from a knowledge creation process in which an enterprise combines both direct experience and trial and error to develop a new service: an enterprise-wide Y2K readiness approach. Most of the secondary sources used for the analysis are from the Shell Oil's web site, Shell's Y2K Survival Guide (1998), Shell's Year 2000 Survival: A Practitioners' Guide (1997), The Year 2000 Problem and the Oil Industry (Miller & Stoddart, 1999) and Shell's SEC report.

Shell is a multinational oil enterprise listed on the New York Stock Exchange (NYSE) with headquarters in the US. Although some of its Y2K publications are dated as early as 1996, it formally initiated its Y2K program in 1997 (Shell's Year, 1998). Shell estimated that it will spend $150 million to identify, analyze, and remediate the Y2K problem (Miller & Stoddart, 1999 p45). In the oil industry, Shell can be considered as one of the early adopters of Y2K solution strategies. Shell had a consultancy team to assess its Y2K risk and identify what is at stake.

After years of substantial investment in its technical infrastructure, Shell's management needed its own operational understanding and approaches to the problem. It recognized the need to contain the impact of Y2K problem for its enterprise-wide operations and ensure business continuity. Shell approached the Y2K problem with the following questions in mind:

- What would happen if Shell (1997, p27) does nothing? In other words, what is at stake?
- How should the enterprise begin to address the problem?
- How should the enterprise organize and manage its Y2K approach?
- What operational pieces of knowledge are needed to resolve the problem? These pertain to Y2K definition, inventory of IT systems, risk assessment, date standard, outsourcing guidelines, remediation option, and due diligence approach.

Appendix F expands on Shell's needs, Y2K project process, due diligence approach, and generation of Y2K intellectual capital (IC). Intellectual capital is intellectual material that has been formalized, captured, and leveraged to produce a higher-valued asset (Stewart, 1997).

Shell formalized, captured, and created Y2K knowledge that has been converted into tangible and intangible assets. Some of the tangible assets are listed in Appendix F while the intangible ones include their experiences and know-how in managing the Y2K problem. For Shell, management can measure the flow of new Y2K ideas from people, the social interaction, and the shaping of the ideas into new products such as Y2K Survival Guide. By sharing its Y2K tangible informational assets, Shell contributed to the increase in how-to information about the problem.

Expanding Community of Y2K Specialists (*Period 3, 1997 - 1999, August.*)

With more enterprises becoming active in Y2K remediation activities, Y2K experiences, knowledge, uncertainty, cost, and IT failures were expanding. Litigation cases were filed by clients whose systems failed or shareholders of IT enterprises. More Y2K software patches were being released by an expanding, international community of Y2K vendors.

With increasing legal, regulatory, and industry pressures for enterprises to report their status of Y2K readiness, their Y2K teams became multi-disciplinary with members coming from different units. For example, Shell's Y2K teams may include technical specialists, accountant, public relations coordinator, lawyer, tax consultant, insurance, and outsource specialists (see Appendix F).

Members of the enterprise's Y2K task force had to develop background knowledge on Y2K issues related to their disciplines. Therefore, the members probably became active in identifying internal and external resources and using approaches that Huber (1991) classified as knowledge acquisition, information distribution and information interpretation. For example, Y2K issues for the accountancy profession, like accounting for software conversion costs, materiality, and disclosure are disseminated in their professional publications, Y2K accountant conferences, on-line discussion forums, and web sites. Accountancy related web sites provided access to resources such as:

- The Responsibilities of Auditors with Respect to Y2K (www.bus.orst.edu/faculty/BROWNC/Year2000/more_y2k.htm),
- The American Institute of Certified Public Accountants (AICPA) Y2K Auditing Guidance (www.aicpa.org/members/y2000/intro.htm), and
- The British Standards Institution (BSI) definition of Year 2000 (www.llgm.com/FIRM/article1.htm).

To support informal intellectual disclosure and the sharing of Y2K information, computer-mediated social groups known as virtual communities started to evolve. Organizations and individuals including deJager sponsored hundreds of Y2K newsgroups, listservs (mailing lists), and virtual conferences. Their activities resemble the San Francisco Bay Area's WELL (Whole Earth 'Lectronic Link). The WELL is a computer conference system that enables people around the world to carry on public conversation and exchange email (Rheingold, 1993; Hagel & Armstrong, 1997, p ix). It nurtures a loose flow of information, reciprocity relationships, virtual connections, and informal exchange.

As people exchanged information, specific Y2K researchers, organizations, and web sites are mentioned in different messages. People are giving their comments and redundant information is starting to emerge. There are about 100 Y2K on-line discussion forums such as:

- comp.software.year-2000,
- alt.talk.year2000,
- Compuserve Y2K special interest group, and
- Year 2000 Discussion List at www.year2000.com/y2kmaillist.html.

The Year 2000 Information Center (www.year2000.com/y2kusergroups.html) provides a geographic and subject list of newsgroups.

The Y2K on-line discussion forums are becoming subjects for analyzing sociometric data (who cites whom) and identifying redundancy. The data are being used to analyze relevancy and the strength of ties within Y2K social networks. For example, a comprehensive Y2K web site for laypersons is North's (www.garynorth.com) (Yourdon & Yourdon, 1999). The controversial web site provides analysis and opinion as well as links to full-text background resources.

A recent online search of com.software.year-2000 newsgroup for comments (within the last month) about North (www.garynorth.com) resulted in 129 messages. The search tool, DejaNews, allows for tracking message threads so the messages can be analyzed and downloaded by topics. In addition, Deja News provides the capability of tracking individual author's past messages and downloading each message. This provides the capability of capturing data about a team member's Y2K network links as well as full-text of the informal comments.

Although researchers have analyzed online discussion forums (Denzin, 1999; Hahn & Stout, 1994), currently none have focused on Y2K virtual communities. Within the Y2K environment, illustrative points of interest include queries such as:

- Who are people citing in their Y2K publications? Why?
- How are they finding out about what does and does not work?
- What are the characteristics of Y2K virtual teams in comparison with other virtual teams?

- What are the opinions regarding the latest predictions such as Y2K conspiracy and espionage?

Another aspect of developing team knowledge is redundancy. According to Nonaka (1994 p25), interpersonal communication among team members from different units is assisted by some degree of redundant information. Solving complex problems is made possible when its members share redundant information that enables them to enter another person's area and provide advice. Redundant information determines the extent to which new perspectives are diffused such as the BSI Definition of Year 2000 compliance. Using a web linkage search, BSI's definition has appeared on about 135 web sites including, but not necessarily limited to:

- 110 enterprises' web sites such as Cisco (y2k.k12.ut.us/cisco.htm),
- Twelve discipline-specific web site such as the law firm of Leboeuf, Lamb, Greene & MacRae (www.llgm.com/FIRM/article1.htm), and
- Six international organizations web sites such as the World Bank (www.worldbank.org/infodev/y2k/toolkit/Resources.htm).

The enterprises' web sites provide compliance information and state that they follow the definition of Y2K compliance provided by BSI. In several countries, the BSI definition is being used as a benchmark for product compliance (Kenney & Gerwinat, 1999 p5). Since there is no universally accepted definition of Y2K compliance, it would be interesting to find out how many enterprises use alternative definitions of Y2K provided by other organizations like the ITAA (www.itaa.org/year2000).

The diffusion of the BSI definition supports a team's efforts to create or agree upon an organizational definition of Y2K. Information redundancy is an enabling condition for organizational knowledge creation and can lead to the sharing of personal (tacit) knowledge (Nonaka, 1994 p29). Also, information redundancy is evident in the duplicate publishing of Jones' (1996) Global Economic Impact of the Year 2000 and deJager's (1993) Doomsday as well as the hundreds of web sites that are linked to deJager's Year 2000 Information Center (www.year2000.com).

The web sites such as US State Department, Accounting for the Year 2000 Problem, and the Legal Services Corporation which have hypertext links to deJager's site are recommending his site to their audiences. Therefore, Y2K task force members from the legal, accounting and technical departments (units) within an enterprise are being exposed and introduced to the same Y2K resources. Later, the resources may be analyzed, evaluated, and disseminated to others. Also, they may be uploaded to the enterprise's Y2K Intranet (in-house Internet) to be shared with the in-house Y2K task force and cited in their specialized reports.

Information Sharing *(Period 3, 1997 - 1999, August.)*

deJager's Year 2000 Information Center and Shell Oil's full-text publications are examples of information sharing (www.shell.com.my). Both have made substantial contributions to the global creation and sharing of Y2K resources. In Shell's Y2K publications, they cite how other enterprises, such as the British Standard Institute (BSI), are freely providing technical information on topics such as the definition of Y2K compliance, list of dates for inclusion in testing schedule, testing and evaluation procedures, and Y2K solution vendor databases (Shell, 1998).

International organizations such as the World Bank (1998) also stress the importance of information sharing in their report on how to develop a national Y2K project. The report outlines several procedures for disseminating Y2K information such as:

- Distribute Y2K documents and survey results,
- Establish and maintain a national Y2K web site,
- Coordinate and publicize Y2K forums, seminars and national recruitment drives,
- Prepare and disseminate monthly progress reports, and
- Disseminate Y2K national plans.

As illustrated above, widespread sharing of information about experiences with national Y2K projects, project management, system testing, compliance, and failed approaches is essential. Unfortunately, some enterprises have either been reluctant or unable to share their experiences with suppliers, customers, and competitors. Many customers have turned to the vendors of their systems that can not be easily tested for information about compliance status. Those vendors, however, have come up empty (Zerega, 1998). Some vendors are providing compliance statements that are constantly changing as new problems are identified in testing.

Legislation and Internet

Enterprises have become concerned with liabilities because some vendors are already facing litigation, such as the first reported Y2K lawsuit - Produce Palace International vs. TEC-America Cash Register, Inc. (Nadler & Fong, n.d.). In testimony before the U.S. House of Representatives Science Committee, in March 1997, Ann Coffou, a Managing Director of the Giga Information Group, estimated that Year

2000 litigation cost could reach or even exceed $1 trillion (Jinnett, July 1997).

To stimulate the sharing of information, several governments have enacted national Y2K legislation. Appendix C identifies the "Good Samaritan" legislations introduced in the US, Australia, and New Zealand. In the US, the Year 2000 Information Readiness and Disclosure Act (IRDA) was enacted on October 19, 1998. Its purpose is to encourage business-to-business communication on readiness assessments, tools, strategies, and other information related to Y2K remediation efforts (www.itaa.org/year2000/irdaguide.htm). The Act protects enterprises against the use in any civil litigation of technical Y2K information about an enterprise's experiences with effecting product compliance, system fixes, testing procedures and results, when those information are disclosed in good faith.

According to analysts, the Act will likely be significant for owners of computer equipment because the computer industry has not been very proactive in notifying consumers of potential Y2K problems or recalling products (Zerega, 1998). Often, this is compared to the practice by automobile and appliance manufacturers that proactively notify consumers of defects in their products. Zerega also noted other analysts who disagreeingly state that removing vendor liability, in an effort to motivate information sharing, may benefit vendors more than users. Isfahani, an industry analyst at the Giga Information Group, added that the Act is letting vendors say something that may not be true without having to take responsibility for it (Zerega, 1998).

In particular, the Act supports the information sharing via the Internet. To promote cooperation among enterprises in the same industry, the Act provides a limited, temporary exception from the US antitrust laws. In support of the Act, the President's Council on Year 2000 Conversion provides suggestions on how to use the Internet for the sharing of Y2K information (www.y2k.gov/new/share.html). The Council works with several industry groups to develop strategies for building Y2K databases (Opportunity, n.d.).

The actions of the Council in recommending the use of the Internet for information sharing is in line with the global trends of sharing Y2K information via the Net. According to Jones (1998, p157), the Year 2000 problem is the first major business issue to occur during the explosive growth of the Internet and near-universal usage of email functions.

Kurland's (1997) study of the Internet and Y2K information reported that the web, mailing lists and newsgroups have become major tools for the sharing of Y2K information and the search for the "magic bullet" solution. Although no "magic bullet" or "silver bullet" has been found, a diversity of resources has become available including survivalist (how to survive the Y2K problem), ranking, and survey resources. A highly recommended survivalist site is available at www.cassandraproject.org.

An interesting aspect of manyY2K surveys is that the survey questionnaire and associated answers as well as the report are provided full-text via Internet. To track Y2K progress over time, many associations and research groups such as Business Strategies and Neaman Bond Associates have conducted a series of surveys. For example, Viasoft commissioned Neaman Bond Associates, a British consulting firm, to conduct studies to see how European firms are preparing themselves for the Euro and Y2K conversions (Wilson, 1997; Year 2000 in). In the 1997 study, the findings indicate many of the respondents were focusing more resources on the Euro problem than the Y2K problem. The results are available full-text in portable document format (PDF). About two dozen surveys and their web addresses are identified in the Y2K chronology. The chronology in Excel format is available on request.

Figure 11 provides a schematic overview of how the Internet is being used to support the sharing of Y2K information. In the diagram, enterprises use Internet resources such as web sites, file transfer protocol (FTP) sites, online discussion forums, and email for communication and information access. The enterprises load information a.k.a. Y2K artifacts about their Y2K readiness, product compliance, and project planning approaches on the Net to inform the public and stakeholders of such efforts.

For example, Shell provides access to several Y2K information artifacts such as a checklist, initiation plan template, sample compliance letter, and Y2K Survival Guide. To facilitate the use of the resources, Shell even provides those resources in a portable document format (PDF). Unfortunately, the content of the PDF file is 'invisible' to most search engines so many users are unaware of the full text resources that are available at Y2K web sites. Since PDF documents are compressed (zipped up) files, their contents are not indexed full text in most search engines such as Alta Vista, Hot Bot, and Excite.

In addition to loading Y2K information, the Internet provides a platform for testing customized services such as:

- Current awareness notification of changes in products (www.infoliant.com),
- Database of vendor compliance statements (www.vendor2000.com),
- Publishing and marketing your own Y2K book in paperback and PDF formats such as WHY 2K? (www.upublish.com/books/reid.htm),

- Database for tracking failures of embedded systems, and
- Artificial intelligence agent for tracking Y2K compliance statements at Y2K web sites and SEC statements (millie.y2klinks.com/html/MillieFrame.htm).

Figure 11 - Using Internet to Support Y2K

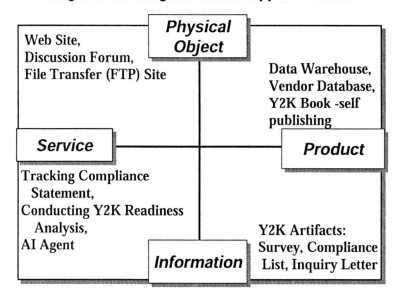

Some enterprises design the Internet and Intranet (in-house Internet) services to support the due diligence process such as a data warehouse about their Y2K program. Figure 12 provides an illustration of the phased approach. Figure 13 applies the phased approach to the due diligence process. The due diligence process and the phased approach are examined and illustrated in several publications (Gordon, 1997 p76; Shell, 1997).

With the requirements of due diligence, the government financial disclosure requirement, and increasing public awareness, more Y2K information has become available. New obstacles are surfacing in the area of information overload, reliability, and accuracy. In the Year 2000 Discussion Forum (year2000-discuss@year-2000.com), subscribers are posting messages in which they are asking for solutions to the information overload and quality control problems. In fact, a report by the US Senate Special Committee on Year 2000 Problem (Investigating, 1999, p1) highlights that

> "The most frustrating aspect of addressing the Y2K problem is sorting fact from fiction. The Internet surges with rumors of massive Y2K test failures that turn out to be gross misstatements, while image-sensitive enterprises downplay real Y2K problems".

With almost universal access to Internet, it became a major tool for sharing Y2K information.

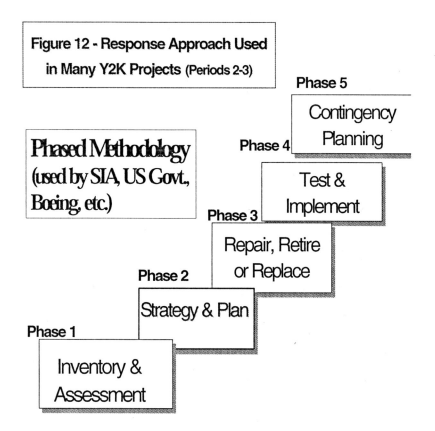

Figure 12 - Response Approach Used in Many Y2K Projects (Periods 2-3)

Phased Methodology (used by SIA, US Govt., Boeing, etc.)

Phase 1
Inventory & Assessment

Phase 2
Strategy & Plan

Phase 3
Repair, Retire or Replace

Phase 4
Test & Implement

Phase 5
Contingency Planning

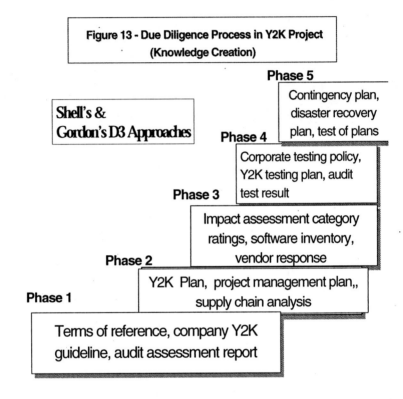

Figure 13 - Due Diligence Process in Y2K Project (Knowledge Creation)

Chapter 7: Legal Activities in Y2K

As more enterprises became involved in Y2K efforts and media attention continued to focus on the problem, it became clearer to the US Congress that disclosure of Year 2000 readiness information is only a part of the Y2K problem solution (Investigating 1999, p135). Since many businesses will not be able to complete their remediation work in time, they are likely to experience Y2K related failures. In such a global economy, one enterprise's inability to fulfill its contractual obligation may have a domino effect on the operation of its upstream and downstream partners. This may result in more enterprises seeking recourse through the courts.

As mentioned earlier, Coffou's prediction that litigation costs arising out of Y2K problem could at least be $1 trillion has created a great deal of interest. Because of the uncertainty associated with the problem, it is getting much attention from the popular press, lawyers, senior managers, software and hardware providers, the US Congress, and others with interests in the IT industry. As a result, numerous articles have been published surmising that substantial litigation will be produced as a byproduct of the Y2K problem (Jinnett, 1997 p15). Web sites such as Y2K Liability (www.2000law.com), Year 2000 Law Bytes (www.year2000.com/lawcenter/lawbytes.html), and Alan Simpson's ComLinks.com (www.comlinks.com) are on the increase. The Y2K Liability web site provides full-text access to Y2K Congressional testimony, US legislation and litigation.

These developments have also resulted in law firms such as Thelen, Reid & Priest in San Francisco, training lawyers to become Y2K savvy (Feder, 1999d). Lawyers are asking questions about when enterprises became aware of the two-digit date problem, and monitoring legislative activities to see if governments will introduce new laws to cap Y2K liabilities.

Since some enterprises are concentrating on their Y2K remediation efforts, others are focusing their energies on the legal process to assist in resolving their Y2K problems. The following section describes three major legal responses to Y2K: litigation, legislation, and alternative dispute resolution.

Response - Lawsuits

Some say that more than 50 lawsuits have been filed in the US, mostly by small companies whose software programs failed (Legislation, 1999). The Y2K Liability web site identifies 71 legal cases filed in US. In addition, there has been much speculation as to the types of legal cases surrounding Y2K. For example, Jones (1996), Steinberg and Pegalis (n.d.) have created categories for grouping potential Y2K litigation. In 1996, Jones (www.spr.com/html/year_2000_problem.htm) has identified at least six types of potential Y2K litigation such as the class action litigation filed by affected customers of software packages (see Chapter 3).

Steinberg and Pegalis (www.comlinks.com/legal/ste1.htm) created a working taxonomy of the potential Y2K litigation. The taxonomy is organized by computer platforms such as: mainframe customer v. manufacturers; network and PC customers v. manufacturers; and customers v. software manufacturers.

In the US the first lawsuit, Produce Palace International v. TEC-America Cash Register (Japan), and All American Cash Register, Inc., was filed in 1997 and involved a Michigan grocery store (Grossman, 1998). The grocery sued because the system it purchased in 1995 had been repeatedly interrupted by the failure of a computerized checkout scanning system to process credit cards with expirations dates such as 2000 and beyond.

According to the plaintiff's attorney, the parties agreed on July 29, 1998 to enter state-sponsored mediation, averting a September trial date (Zerega, 1999). In the settlement reached in November 1998, the vendor paid Produce Palace $250,000 (Feder, 1999d). Feder describes it as the first case to result in a settlement paying damages to a plaintiff.

The next case was the first Y2K class action lawsuit, Atlaz International v. Software Business Technologies, Inc. (SBT) filed in December 1997 in California. Nadler and Fong (n.d.) described a class action lawsuit as one in which an individual plaintiff seeks to represent the interests of many other similarly situated persons or enterprises, such as all those who purchased the same defective product.

In Atlaz, the suit seeks to represent all persons or enterprises that purchased the SBT Pro Series accounting software before March 1, 1997 (Nadler & Fong, n.d.). According to the complaint, the defendant sold software version 3.0i that was not Year 2000 compliant. In March 1997, SBT released an "upgrade" version of the software that is compliant. The complaint contains counts for breach of warranty, fraud and deceit, and unfair business practices under California laws. The plaintiffs seek damages over $50 million. The class action plaintiffs alleged that SBT is improperly forcing customers to pay hefty fees to correct Y2K problem (Nadler & Fong, n.d.).

In more recent lawsuits, major vendors, such as IBM, AT&T, and Lucent Technologies, Inc., have joined the ranks of those being sued for not forewarning customers that the equipment they sold in recent years can not handle Year

2000 dates and for not supplying free upgrades (Feder, 1999d).

Recently, GTE, a regional phone carrier in the US, filed a historical Y2K lawsuit against five insurance enterprises seeking $400 million to cover its repair expenditures (Feder, 1999b). According to Feder, it is believed to be the first lawsuit to test whether insurers may be compelled to pay for some of expenses in Y2K repair work.

For trends in international cases, regulations, and legal interpretations emerging elsewhere in the world, consult Kenney and Gerwinat's article (1999).

Response - Legislation

With the current increase in lawsuits and the prospect of substantial litigation, the US Congress became concerned. From the first hearing of the US Senate Special Committee on Year 2000 Problem, the litigation issue has been discussed (Investigating, 1999 p 135). Since industry leaders, business leaders and Y2K experts have expressed concern about litigation, the US Congress recently passed legislation that caps Y2K liability. The Act, signed by President Clinton in July 1999, caps punitive damages at $250,000, limits attorneys' fees, and promotes federal loans to small businesses to fix the problem before the end of the year (Clinton, 1999; Legislation, 1999). It gives offending enterprises 90 days to fix problems to ward off a lawsuit.

Already, there has been much debate about how the new legislation will impact on GTE's Y2K lawsuit against five insurance enterprises (Feder, 1999b). It has been a topic on the online discussion forum of the Practicing Lawyers Institute Y2K Legal Forum (pli-y2klaw@pli.edu).

Thus far, the US is the only national government that has passed Y2K liability legislation. According to Kenney and Gerwinat (1999 p2), "On the whole, foreign governments and courts have been disinclined to treat Y2K as an extraordinary circumstance requiring new legal rules".

Response - Alternative Dispute Resolution

Some enterprises are being proactive in the Y2K litigation area in case they are sued (Y2K: Who's, 1998). They are participating in a dispute resolution program spearheaded by the Information Technology Association of America (ITAA). The objective of the program is to secure pledges from enterprises to mediate and negotiate Y2K disputes before resorting to the courts. The former is precisely the objective of the Millennium Accord, which sets up principles and procedures to prevent or resolve millennium-bug-related disputes (year2000.dci.com/Articles/990203mediation.htm). It was unveiled in early December at the Centre for Dispute Resolution (CDR) in the UK. Led by alternative dispute resolution bodies, the Accord has been launched in Singapore, Hong Kong and Australia. In Singapore, the Singapore Mediation Centre, a subsidiary of the Singapore Academy of Law, leads it.

For enterprises that are interested in dispute resolution, several studies provide procedures for building Y2K alternative dispute resolution (ADR) programs. Goldberg (1998) and Radosevich (1998) provide overviews of how to approach ADR.

In hindsight, and based on the foregoing events, the use of legal recourse to address the issue of who is liable to pay for costs of making products and/or services Y2K compliant is being avoided in favor of out-of-court settlements. The last two modes of 'responses' appear to be the result of a tight balancing act by the government (US) to safeguard both the interests of the IT industry and the enterprises. Whether this 'constrained optimum' will be the norm in the future will depend on the preparations put in place by industry players so as to keep the quantum of losses at reduced levels.

Chapter 8: Conclusion

As illustrated in Figure 2, the Y2K remediation approach begun with pre-contemplation at various starting points during the first period (1960-1991) with limited commitments. In Period 2 (1992-1996), some action and preparations became visible. It was not until Period 3 (1997-1999) that more concrete and definitive responses took shape. This last period saw the various segments of the global society taking on a more serious view of the problem with the objective of resolving it. In addition, heads of governments became actively involved in taking a handle of what was seen as a globally threatening situation. It became apparent that non-action or allowing market forces on their own to resolve the Y2K problem will not suffice because of the high level of 'interconnectedness' of entire economies and business activities. In the US, laws were enacted to provide the backbone for enforcing both mandatory requirements as well as ensuring that all sectors of society are adequately protected from potentially devastating results.

Large enterprises, dominated by the financial sector, were among the first to deploy resources to resolve the Y2K problem area. They turned to knowledge creation and self-help strategies to ensure business continuity in the next millennium. Small and medium scale enterprises (SMEs), which either purchased off-the-shelf systems applications and hardware or outsource the development of their computer-based information systems, needed to depend on the solutions or fixes by vendors and outsourcers.

Like the plight of the SMEs, governments of developing nations needed to turn to international bodies like the UN, World Bank and APEC for both financial and technical knowledge to address counterpart situations in their countries.

A truly concerted and globally coordinated approach has been the hallmark for resolving a problem originally thought to be technical in nature. Money is no longer the overriding concern, rather it is ensuring that the global community's businesses and services usher in the new millenium minus the disruptions and chaotic events forecasted if the world did not act in time.

In summary, the resolution and global recognition of the harmful effects of failing to address the Y2K problem has led to international cooperation and collaboration among government officials, legislators, association leaders, managers, and competitors. These entities are sharing resources and working together to support the resolution of the problem and ensure public safety. Their activities have resulted in a diversity of responses to the Y2K problem, community of Y2K specialists, new knowledge about the problem, and increased social interaction and networking. As a result of these activities, the Y2K problem area has evolved into three periods, namely: Period 1, 1960-1991, Period 2, 1992-1996, and Period 3, 1997-1999. A fourth period commencing on the 1st of January 2000 will demonstrate further the global extent of the problem.

This Y2K study utilized a framework for the analysis of contemporary global issues in a networked environment. Based on a knowledge discovery approach, it tested a framework for identifying social networks, key moments in the history of emerging communities, flow of information as it spreads through social systems, and intellectual/social maps of the Y2K remediation efforts. With the current limitations on diffusion and knowledge creation studies, the study provides an illustration of the importance of the Internet as a multifaceted medium for analyzing the ongoing and dynamic spread of a new contemporary issue and how knowledge is created.

With the increasing demands, complexity, time limitation, and uncertainty associated with the Y2K problems, the Y2K community would not have had time to respond to request for surveys, interviews or on-site observations as techniques for data collection. Therefore, the use of archival and current resources in print, electronic and multimedia formats became an excellent alternative approach for collecting data on the ongoing spread of the Y2K problem. Furthermore, the study provided an opportunity to use the Internet for electronic monitoring, tracing, validating and analyzing Y2K events. As a result, a chronology of about 130 Y2K events is identified. Since the chronology (Appendix A) is available in Excel format, it can function as a living chronology that is updated and customized for your needs.

References

Almind, T.C., & Ingwersen, P., 1997. Informetric Analyses on the World Wide Web: Methodological Approaches to Webiometrics. *Journal of Documentation*, v.53 #4, p404-426.

Bemer, Bob, 1971. What's the Date? *Honeywell Computer Journal*, v.4, p205,208.

Business Strategies Ltd., 1999. On Course ... Or Too Late. Year 2000 Survey (2) June 1999. (www.taskforce2000.co.uk)

Butt, Robert, 1998. The Australian Government's Strategy for the Millennium Bug. GB& ICA Workshop, 29-30 June, 1998.

Cairncross, Frances, 1998. Survey the Millennium Bug. Time Runs Out. *Economist*, 19 September 1998. (www.economist.com/editorial/freeforall/19-9-98/bug1.html)

Chng, Grace, 1999. A Cooperative Effort to Tackle the Bug. ComputerTimes (*The Straits Times*), 5 May 1999.

Clinton Signs Y2K Law Protecting Companies, 1999. Reuters, 20 July 1999. (www.techweb.com/wire/story/reuters/REU19990720S0003)

Cohen, Bob, 1997. ITAA's Year 2000 Outlook. In Leon Kappelman, *Year 2000 Problem: Strategies & Solutions from the Fortune 100.* p.230-239, International Thomson Computer Press

Computerworld, 1998. Case Study of six companies (not exact title). *Computerworld*, 12 January 1998, March 1998, June 1998, October 1998, February 1999. (www.computerworld.com)

Computing SA (world-online.net/project2000/north/206.htm). Chris Anderson (www.y2ktimebomb.com/Bios/cabio.htm);

Craig, Andrew, 1997. US Leads Millennium Awareness, Survey Says. TechWeb. 4 December 1997. (www.techweb.com)

deJager, Peter, 1993. Doomsday 2000. *Computerworld*. September 1993. (www.year2000.com/archive).

deJager, Peter, 1996. Unjustified Optimism. Testimony before House of Representatives, Testimony to Science Committee, 14 May 1996. (www.year2000.com/archive/testimony.html)

deJager, Peter and Bergeon, Richard, 1999. *Countdown Y2K: Business Survival Planning for the Year 2000*, Wiley.

deJager, Peter and Bergeon, Richard, 1997. *Managing 00 Surviving the Year 2000 Computing Crisis*, Wiley.

Diederich, Tom, 1998. SEC Sets Y2K Guidelines. *Computerworld*. July 1998. (www.computerworld.com/home/news.nsf/idgnet/980731sec)

DiMaggio, Paul J., and Powell, Walter W., 1983. The Iron Cage Revisited: Institutional Isomorphism and Collective Rationality in Organizational Fields. *American Sociological Review*, v. 48 April 1983. p147-160.

Feder, Barnaby J., 1988. For Computers, the Year 2000 May Prove a Bit Traumatic. *The New York Times*, 7 May 1988.

Feder, Barnaby J., 1999a. Counting to 2000: Betting on a Bug as the Clock Nears Midnight. *The New York Times*, 15 July 1999.

Feder, Barnaby J., 1999c. Gartner, an Early Y2K Analyst, Dominates the Niche. *The New York Times*, 5 July 1999.

Feder, Barnaby J., 1999b. GTE Sues Over Y2K Repairs. *The New York Times*. 1 July 1999. (search.nytimes.com)

Feder, Barnaby J., 1999d. Lawsuits Related to Y2K Problem Start Trickling Into the Courts. *The New York Times*, 12 April 1999.

Feder, Barnaby J., 1998. The Town Crier for the Year 2000. *The New York Times*, 11 October 1998.

Gelfond, Susan M., 1988. Are Computers Headed for Panic in the Year 2000. *Business Week*, 4 April 1988.

Gelinas, Ulrich J., Sutton, Steve G., and Oram, Allan E., 1999. *Accounting Information Systems*. 4th edition. South-Western College Publishing.

Gillin, Paul, 1998. A Y2K Pioneer Seeks (and deserves) Recognition. *Computerworld*, 3 August 1998. (www.computerworld.com/home/features.nsf/idgnet/980803 gillin)

Gillin, Paul, 1984. The Problem You May Not Know You Have. *Computerworld*, 13 February 1984. (www.computerworld.com/home/features.nsf/all/980803sch oen)

Goldberg, Steven H., 1998. Building Corporate Y2K ADR Programs. Countdown 2000 (Lexis Law Publishing), December 1998.

Gordon, Steven R., 1997. Corporate Due Diligence for the Year 2000 Problem. In Leon Kappelman, *Year 2000 Problem: Strategies & Solutions from the Fortune 100.* p.76-87, International Thomson Computer Press.

Grossman, Mark, 1998. Protecting Your Company from Y2K Related Litigation. (www.y2ktimebomb.com/Litigation/mgross9829a.htm)

GTE Sues to Recover Y2K Costs, 1999. *Information Week,* 2 July 1999. (www.informationweek.com/story/IWK19990702S0005)

Hagel, John and Armstrong, Arthur G., 1997. Net.gain: Expanding Markets Through Virtual Communities. Harvard Business School Press.

Huber, George P., 1991. Organizational Learning: the Contributing Processes and the Literatures. *Organization Science* v.2 #1, February 1991. P88-115.

Investigating the Impact of the Year 2000 Problem, 1999. US Senate, S. Prt.106-10, February, 1999. (www.access.gpo.gov/congress/senate/sp106-10.html)

Jackson, Michele H., 1997. Assessing the Structure of Communication on the World Wide Web. JCMC, v.3 #1, June 1997. (www.ascusc.org/jcmc/vol3/issue1/jackson.html)

Jinnett, Jeff, 1997. Testimony - Jeff Jinnett before the US Senate Banking, Housing and Urban Affairs Committee,

Subcommittee on Financial Services and Technology, 10 July 1997. (www.comlinks.com/gov/jin710.htm)

Jinnett, Jeff, 1997. Legal Issues Confronting the Federal and State Governments Due to the Year 2000 "Millennium Bug" Problem, June 1997. (www.comlins.com); (www.year2000.com/archive/Nflegalissues.html)

Johnson, Jerry L., Rosmond, Kathy and Kappelman, Leon A., 1997. Year 2000 and the Role of Government. In Leon Kappelman, *Year 2000 Problem: Strategies & Solutions from the Fortune 100.* p.225-228, International Thomson Computer Press. (www.year2000.unt.edu/kappelma/y2kgov.htm)

Jones, Capers, 1997. The Emergence of the Year 2000 Repair Industry. Wilson, Tim, 1997. Year 2000 Issue Takes a Backseat Overseas. Techweb, 8 December 1997. (www.techweb.com)

Jones, Capers, 1996. The Global Economic Impact of the Year 2000 Software Problem. Software Productivity Research, Inc. (SPR). (www.spr.com/library/)

Jones, Capers, 1997b. The Global Economic Impact of the Year 2000 Problem. In Leon Kappelman, *Year 2000 Problem: Strategies & Solutions from the Fortune 100.* p.12-29, International Thomson Computer Press.

Jones, Capers, 1998. *The Year 2000 Software Problem: Quantifying the Costs and Assessing the Consequences,* Addison-Wesley.

Kappelman, Leon A., 1999. "Message Regarding Your June 11 Posting to Year 2000 Listserv". 18 June 1999 16:46:38 – 0500.

Kappelman, Leon A. and Cappel, James, 1996. Confronting the Year 2000 Issue. *Journal of Systems Management*, Jul/Aug 1996. Vol. 47 #4. (www.comlinks.com/mag/cirep.htm)

Kappelman, Leon A. and Cappel, James, 1996. Overcoming Year 2000 Avoidance. In Leon Kappelman, *Year 2000 Problem: Strategies & Solutions from the Fortune 100.* p.58-62, International Thomson Computer Press.

Kappelman, Leon A., Fent, Darla and Prybutok, Victor R., 1997. How Much Will Year 2000 Compliance Cost? In Leon Kappelman, *Year 2000 Problem: Strategies & Solutions from the Fortune 100.* p.279-290, International Thomson Computer Press.

Kappelman, Leon A. and Keppel, Kellie B., 1997. Report on the Year 2000 Problem: A Benchmarks and Status Study. In Leon Kappelman, *Year 2000 Problem: Strategies & Solutions from the Fortune 100.* p.264-278, International Thomson Computer Press.

Kenney, Robert J. and Gerwinat, Stefan, 1999. What's Happening Overseas? LegalTimes.com, 6 December 1999. (www.legaltimes.com/expcfm/display.cfm?id=2314)

Kucera, Kenneth M., 1997. They Created Their Own Solution: Smart Bridging. In Leon Kappelman, *Year 2000 Problem: Strategies & Solutions from the Fortune 100.* p.206-209, International Thomson Computer Press.

Larsen, Ray, 1996. Bibliometrics of the World Wide Web. (Sherlock.berkeley.edu/asis96/node1.html)

Legislation Aims to Keep Y2K Bug Out of the Courtroom, 1999. CNN Interactive, 23 February, 1999. (www.cnn.com/TECH/computing/9902/23/y2k.legislation/

Marcoccio, Lou, 1998. Year 2000 Global State of Readiness and Risks to the General Business Community. Expert Testimony of Lou Marcoccio (Gartner Group) to the US Senate Special Committee on the Year 2000 Technology Problem, 7 October, 1998, Washington, D.C.

Marcoccio, Lou, 1999. Year 2000 World Status Update. Gartner Group, 14 April 1999.

McKendrick, Joseph, 1997. Impact of the Year 2000 and IBM Midrange Systems. In Leon Kappelman, *Year 2000 Problem: Strategies & Solutions from the Fortune 100.* p.251-256, International Thomson Computer Press.

Meador, C. Lawrence and Freeman, Leland, 1997. Year 2000: the Domino Effect. *Datamation,* January 1997.

Miller, Keith and Stoddart, Simon, 1999. The Year 2000 Problem and the Oil Industry. Presented at APEC Y2K Symposium, 22-23 April 1999, Singapore. International Energy Agency (IEA), 1999.

Nadler, David M. and Fong, Kendrick C. First Year 2000 Class Action Filed. Comlinks.com. (www.comlinks.com/legal/dmm3.htm)

Nonaka, Ikujiro, 1994. A Dynamic Theory of Organizational Knowledge Creation. *Organization Science,* v.5 #1, February 1994. p14-37.

Nunno, Richard M., 1999. The Year 2000 Computer Problem: Congressional Issues. Congressional Research Service (CRS), Library of Congress, 19 March 1999. Order Code IB07036. (See Appendix D)

O'Leary, Mick, 1999. Portal Wars. *Online*, Jan/Feb 1999. (www.onlineinc.com)

Opportunity for Industry Associations: Web-Based Year 2000 Information Sharing. President's Council on Year 2000 Conversion. (www.y2k.ov/new/share.htm).

Porter, Patrick L. and Radcliff, Deborah, 1997. Time Bomb. In Leon Kappelman, *Year 2000 Problem: Strategies & Solutions from the Fortune 100.* p.240-247, International Thomson Computer Press.

Prochaska, James O., DiClemente, Carlo C., and Norcross, John C., 1992. In Search of How People Change: Applications to Addictive Behaviors. *American Psychologist*, v. 47 #9, September 1992. p1102-1114.

Radosevich, Lynda. Y2K Legal Games Begin. *InfoWorld*, May 1998.

Reed, Tamara, 1999. Y2K Files. Mixed Messages: A Glance at Other Nations' Y2K Readiness. San Diego Daily Transcript. 15 March 1999.
(www.sddt.com/files/library/99/03/15/tca.html)

Reid, Edna, 1997. MSC Needs IT Literate Workers. *New Straits Times* (Malaysia), November 1997.

Reid, Edna, 1999. Exploratory Study of the Y2K Problem: Analysis of Diffusion and Knowledge Creation Processes. Presented at Annual Conference of the American Society of Information Science (ASIS), 31 October - 4 November, 1999, Washington, D.C.

Reid, Edna and Bauer, Linda, 1999. Wired Island – Wired World: Marketing Singapore. 1999 Wired World, Tourism Conference, September 1999, Singapore.

Reporting the Future. Y2K Perspectives and Resources for the Media. The Arlington Institute, 1999. (www.Y2KTODAY.com)

Rheingold, Howard, 1993. *The Virtual Community: Homesteading on the Electronic Frontier.* Addison-Wesley, 1993.

Rogers, Everett M., 1995. *Diffusion of Innovations*, 2nd edition. The Free Press, 1995.

Schlingser, Matthew J. and Derrever, Suzette W., 1999. When Did You Know? *Legal Times*, 25 January 1999.

Science and Technology - Second Report, 1998. Year 2000 Problem. UK, House of Commons, Session 1997-98.

Septuagenarian Computer Pioneer Leaves Retirement to Fix Y2K Bug. Bob Bemer's Solution Uses Mainframe Computers to Fix Themselves. *Business Dallas* (Dallas, Texas), November, 1998. (www.bigisoft.com/News_Room/Business_Dallas/business_dallas.htm)

Shell Oil, 1998. Y2K Survival Guide, 1998.

Shell Oil, 1997. Year 2000 Survival: a Practitioners' Guide.

Singapore National Y2K Seminar, 1999. Y2K Facing Up to the Challenge: PSA Corp's Perspective. Seminar held in April 1999, Singapore. (www.ncb.gov.sg)

Small Cause (Survey the Millennium Bug series). *Economist*, 19 September 1998. (www.economist.com/editorial/freeforall/19-9-98/bug2.html).

Steinberg, Dan and Pegalis, Andew M. 10 Litigation Battlegrounds. (www.comlinks.com/legal/stel.htm).

Stewart, Thomas A., 1997. *Intellectual Capital.* Biddles Ltd, UK.

Swaine, Michael, 1998. A Chat With Bob Bemer; Pioneer Programmer Offers Mainframe Year 2000 Solution. *Dr. Dobb's Journal*, v.23 #5, May 1998. p115.

Weill, Peter and Broadbent, Marianne, 1997. *Leveraging the New Infrastructure.* Harvard Business School Press.

White Paper. General Background – Bigisoft. (www.bigisoft.com/News_Room/White_Paper/white_paper. htm)

Wilson, Tim, 1997. Year 2000 Issue Takes a Backseat Overseas. Techweb, 8 December 1997. (www.techweb.com)

World Bank. (www.worldbank.org/infodev/y2k/)

World Bank, 1998. Y2K Toolkit: How to Develop a National Plan for the Year 2000 Problem in Developing Countries. World Bank, November 1998. (www.worldbank.org/infodev/y2k/toolkit)

Y2K: Who's Liable? 1998. *Information Week*, 26 October 1998. (three part series) (www.informationweek.com/706/06iuy2k.htm)

Yardeni, Edward, 1998a. Corporate Disclosure: We Need the Full Monty! Testimony before the Senate Banking Committee, 10 June 1998.
The Impact of the Year 2000 Problem on the Global Food Chain. Testimony before Senate Committee on Agriculture, Nutrition, and Forestry.
(www.yardeni.com/articles.html).

Yardeni, Edward, 1998. Y2K Reporter, December 1998. (www.yardeni.com/y2kreporter.html); (www.yardeni.com/cyber.html).

Yardeni, Edward, 1997. Y2K: We Need Answers. Testimony before Senate Banking Committee, 4 November 1997. (www.yardeni.com/articles.html).
Year 2000 in Euorpe: The Impact & the Imperative for Essential Business Systems, 1997. The Neaman Bond Biannual Research Programme. Sponsored by VIASOFT. (available in PDF)

Year 2000 Problem. J.P. Morgan Securities, Inc. (www.jpmorgan.com/MarketDataInd/Research/Y2Kupdate)

Year 2000 Risk Assessment and Planning for Individuals. Gartner Group. Strategic Analysis Report, 28 October 1998. (gartner5.gartnerweb.com/public/static/home/ 00073955.html)

Yourdon, Edward and Yourdon, Jennifer, 1999. *Time Bomb 2000: Revised & Updated,* Prentice-Hall.

Zarocostas, John, 1999. Asia's Laxity on Y2K Cited as World Supply Problem. *Journal of Commerce Special.* February 1999.
(www.joc.com/issues/990203/tlrade/e29194.htm)

Zerega, Blaise, 1998. Clinton Bill Would Protect Vendors from Y2K Lawsuits. Infoworld Electric. 30 July 1998. (www.infoworld.com).

Appendix A - Chronology of Y2K Related Events

Full-text version of the chronology (Excel format) is available upon request. It contains nine fields including event, year, month, response, named entity, organization type, industry, source, and URL.

Send email to Dr. Edna Reid areid@ntu.edu.sg
In subject line, input "Request for Y2K Chronology". A questionnaire will be sent to you. Upon receipt of the completed questionnaire, the chronology will be sent via email.

Event	Year	Mo.	Response	Source
Banks encountered 2-digit date problems with financial long-term contracts	1970		Mortgate processing - inhouse fix	Kappelman & Cappel 1996, www.comlinks.com/mag/cirep.htm; Marcoccio, 1998.
Article published in trade press - 2 digit date problem	1971		Informed technical readers – 2 digit date problem	Swaine 1998; Kappelman's Email 6/99; Bemer 1998
Article published in trade press - 2 digit date problem	1979	2	Informed technical readers - 2 digit date problem	Schlesinger & Derrever 1999; Kappelman's Email 6/99
Article published in trade press (says 1st article in major news magazine)	1984	2	Informed technical readers. Offered solution. Formed company.	Gillin, 1984; 1998, www.computerworld.com; Schoen's 1999, www.flash.net/~bschoen; Gary North. www.garynorth.com;

Appendix B - Attributes of Early Adopters
(Period 2, 1992-1996)

Attribute	Early Adopter	Example	Source
Reason - initiating Y2K conversion	• Failures of mission critical IT systems • View date problem as matter of survival (K&C) • Advantage	Bank of Boston. Canadian Imperial Bank of Commerce (CIBC). Chase Manhattan. Chubb Group. FINA. Fleet Bank. GTE. Healthsource-Provident. Hughes. Kaiser Permanente. Massachusetts Mutual Life. Nations Bank.	(Bank of Boston) Cohen 1997 p232. Banks deJager & Bergeon, 1997, pxii. (Chase) Porter & Radcliff, 1997 p240; SEC disclosure 10Q Nov 98. (Chubb) Cohen 1997 p230. (CIBC) deJager & Bergeon, 1997, pxii. (FINA) Cohen 1997 p236. (Fleet) deJager & Bergeon, 1997, pxii. (GTE) Kappelman & Cappel, 1996. (Healthsource) Kucera, 1997 p257. (Hughes) Kappelman, 1997 p245; Porter & Radcliff, 1997 p245. (Kaiser) deJager & Bergeon, 1997 pxiii. (Mass.) Kappelman & Cappel, 1996. (Nations Bank) deJager & Bergeon, 1997 pxii.

Date		
	Sun Bank. Union. Unum. Philip Morris.Shell. Texaco	(Shell) deJager & Bergeon, 1997 pxii. (Sun)) deJager & Bergeon, 1997 pxii. (Texaco)) deJager & Bergeon, 1997 pxii. (Union) Cohen 1997 p234; *Computerworld*, Jan 98-Feb 99.
1992-1996	Chase - 1995 launch formal program: Enterprise Year 2000 program). Chubb Group - started pilot project in 1995. City of Phoenix - 1995. FINA - 1995 GTE (1994) - set up conversion project.	See sources listed above.

		Healthsource-Provident -1995 Hughes - 1994. Kaiser Permanente - 1991 set up a team. Union Pacific - 1995.	
Industry	• Electronics • Finance • Health • Insura. • Govt. • Transportation	Bank of Boston (finance). Chase (finance). GTE (phone carrier). Hughes (electronics). Kaiser Permanente (health). Unum Life (insurance).	

Cont - Appendix B

Attribute	Early Adopter	Example	Source
Size; (no. employees)	Large	Chase (68,000 employees) Hughes (85,000 employees)	Porter & Radcliff, 1997 p245
Funding	In-house IT budget	Chase estimated $300 million (update of cost). Hughes estimated $125 million.	(Chase) Yourdon & Yourdon, 1998 p178. (Hughes) Porter & Radcliff, 1997 p246.
Applic. portfolio	Large amount of customized applications	Chase - 400 million & 200 million program instructions, respectively, in their portfolio of computer applications	(Chase) Yourdon & Yourdon, 1998 p176
Technical staff	In-house technical staff. Consultant	GTE appointed high level IS managers to be in charge of project. Hughes uses in-house	deJager & Bergeon, 1997; Cohen, 1997.

	technical staff & outsourcing services. Recruit more programmer. Kaiser Permanente - set up tem 20 consultants & 10 internal staff Massachusetts Mutual Life - hired 3 service providers.	(Bank of Boston) Cohen 1997 p232. (Hughes) ; Porter & Radcliff, 1997 p245. (Kaiser) deJager & Bergeon, 1997 pxiii. (Mass.) Kappelman & Cappel, 1996.
Approach	Variety: • Change date fields • Data windowing • Hybrid	• "Bank of Boston performed date-field expansion; replaced date routines with standard routines; identified logical processes that must be changed; changed programs

to fix the logic problems & test them."

- "Hughes - divided effort between Information Systems & Facilities/Manufacturing."

- "Kaiser Permanente - expanded date fields; added century values to all their current data; backtracked into historical data to add century values; removed queries to hardware manufacturer's date routes & installed their own; created a standard set of date-processing routines & replaced all others with them."

- "Mass. Mutual Life Insurance Co. - appointed a Year 2000 project manager. Hired 3 service providers to implement the project which involves reviewing & making needed changes to company's 45 million lines of code."

Appendix B

Attribute	Early Adopter	Example	Source
Learning style	Learn-by-Doing	See list of early adopters.	
Innovative -ness	Willing to bite the bullet & try to resolve Year 2000 problems. (See comment for CIBC).		deJager & Bergeon, 1997, p82. Porter & Radlcliff, 1997. Cohen, 1997.

Appendix C - Government Y2K Events
(Periods 2-3 1992-1999)

Response	Australia	Singapore	UK	US
Investigate Y2K Problem: - study - potential impact & inter-dependency of systems - hearings	1997 - set up Year 2000 Project Office. Support, advise & ensure uniform effort in addressing problem. Central advisory & coordination role. Surveys - Coopers &	1995 - National Computer Board (NCB) began looking into Y2K issue. Identified course of action: - ensure readiness of key infrastructure systems - create	1998 - set up Year 2000 Team to support Ministerial committee. Ernest & Young report: Critical Infrastructure www.cita.gov.uk/2000/ey_study/ey_menu.htm. Held hearings before Parliament www.citu.gov.uk/2000/. Cap Gemini studies of UK organization's Y2K readiness. DTI Study of Y2K	1995 - interagency committee on Y2K conversion. 1996 Apr - started having congressional hearings on Y2K. General Accounting Office (GAO) reports requested by congressional committees www.gao.gov/y2kr.htm. 1998 established Special Committee on Y2K. Senate report: Investigating the Impact of the Year 2000, Feb 99 www.access.gpo.gov/congress/senate/sp106-10.html. Held many hearings before congressional committees www.crs.loc.gov.

Lybrand Y2K www.au.coo pers.com Australian Bankers Association www.banker s.asn.au	national awareness - promote general understandi ng in industry - exhort testing & contingency planning - enhance public communica tion	readiness (1997).

Appendix C

Response	Australia	Singapore	UK	US
Organize, Coordinate & Monitor **: - govt. readiness - infra-structure activities	Using compliance monitoring framework, report to Cabinet by Minister for Finance & Administration. www.ogit.gov.au/year2000 1998 - formed Year 2000 National Steering Committee.	1996 - NCB, coordinator of national Y2K efforts www.ncb.gov.sg/ncb/yr2000 www.mas.gov.sg/y2000 Using compliance monitoring framework, report to Cabinet by NITC.	1998 - established Year 2000 Ministerial www.ccta.gov.uk/2000/ Action 2000 establish private sector: advise and assess. Have task coordinating independent assessment program; establish assessment standards. Quarterly report - internal compliance program www.cita.gov.uk/2000/who_pres.htm	1997 - Senate Subcommittee on Financial Services & Technology started holding hearings on Y2K in financial sector. www.senate.gov/~y2k 1998 - established Year 2000 Conversion Council - for national Y2K leadership www.y2k.gov

Provide high level advice & lead role in coordination. Also, provide support to SMEs.		

Appendix C

Response	Australia	Singapore	UK	US
Increase Awareness - govt. sector. - private sector, - public.	Y2K awareness information, feedback form, dept progress reports - web site www.ogit.gov.au/year2000 1998-national TV & media advertising campaign. Spent 6 mil to warn private-	1996 - NCB launched Y2K National Awareness Campaign. Y2K awareness information, hotline info, pamphlet, self-survey forms, feedback form, Y2K-In-Action Logo. Critical infrastructur	Y2K awareness information, feedback form, consultant's infrastructure report, - web site www.ccta.gov.uk/200 0/ Establish Media Coordination Unit. Establish Taskforce 2000, a non-profit organization funded by UK government. Taskforce 2000 created web site as gateway to country's Y2K status 195.92.149.132/report/main.shtml	Y2K awareness information, feedback form, agency report card, conferences, several web sites www.y2k.gov Senator Bennett - active in increasing Y2K awareness by holding field hearings (see Table 3), writing op-ed pieces for the *New York Times*, Speaking with CEOs, addressing National Press Club (Investigating, p87).

sector businesses. Australian/NZ standard: Definition Year 2000 Conformity Requirements www.y2kregister.com.au	e progress reports - web site www.ncb.gov.sg/ncb/yr2000 1998 - signed MOU with Government of Australia

Appendix C

Response	Australia	Singapore	UK	US
Provide Funding	Funding - 1998 April - government allocated $127 million to assist agencies with task. Estimated cost - 600 million	Funding - NCB provides grant (LECP) to SMEs; share Y2k professional service with neighboring countries www.ncb.g ov.sg/ncb/yr 2000	Funding - government allocated funds to assist agencies with Y2K. In 1998, Action 2000 program received 17 mil pounds for outreach & publicity. 70 mil pounds to help SMEs address Y2K. Funded "Bug-Busters' program which trained over 30,000 employees from SMEs. www.citu.gov.au/2000 /who_pres.htm Provide 10 mil pounds to World Bank & the	Funding - in 1998 funds were reprogrammed to perform Y2K work & supplemental appropriations were provided for federal agencies (CRS, www.freedom.gov/y2k/resources /crs/ib97036.asp) Small Business Administration (SBA) Y2K loan. International - several countries & World Bank for Y2K - $12 mil www.crs.loc.gov

110

Enacted Legislation	None.	1999 Year 2000 Information Disclosure www.ogit.gov.au/year2000	Computer Millenium Non-Compliance (Contingency Plans) Bill (presented to UK House of Commons on 2nd Feb 1999)	Commonweatlth Secretariat www.citu.gov.uk/2000/who_pres.htm	FY 1997 Omnibus Appropriations Act (funding for DOD). FY 1997 Treasury, Postal Service, & General Government Appropriations Bill (directed OMB to provide cost estimates for Y2K). 1998 Examination parity & Year 2000 Readiness for Financial Institutions Act (extended authority of some regulatories). 1998 Defense Appropriations Act (prohibits DOD from purchasing non-compliant Y2K system). 1998 **Information & Readiness**

		Disclosure Act - encourages companies to disclose information on Y2K readiness www.y2k.gov 1999 **Y2K Liability Act** - limits Y2K liability (cap 250,000). (Nunno, March 1999, pCRS-8)

Appendix D - Congressional Research Service, The Library of Congress

CRS Issue Brief for Congress

Received through the CRS Web

Order Code IB97036

The Year 2000 Computer Problem: Congressional Issues

Updated March 19, 1999

Richard M. Nunno

Resources, Science, and Industry Division

CONTENTS

The Year 2000 Computer Problem: Congressional Issues

SUMMARY

IB97036 03-19-99

CRS-1

MOST RECENT DEVELOPMENTS

Recent year 2000 hearings include the following: February 24, the Senate Armed Services Committee, Readiness and

Management Support Subcommittee hearing on the national security ramifications of the Y2K problem; March 1, the Senate Judiciary Committee hearing on S. 461, Y2K Fairness and Responsibility Act; March 2, the Senate Y2K Committee hearing on the Y2K preparedness of the food industry, March 5 on international Y2K issues, and March 11 on litigation issues associated with the Y2K problem; February 19, the House Committee on Government Reform and Oversight, Subcommittee on the District of Columbia hearing on the District's Y2K preparedness; February 23, the Subcommittee on Postal Service and the Government Management, Information and Technology Subcommittee joint hearing on the Y2K preparedness of the U.S. Postal Service; February 24, the House Ways and Means Committee hearing on selected federal agency Y2K conversion efforts and implications for beneficiaries and taxpayers; March 2, the House Science Committee, Technology Subcommittee and the Government Management, Information and Technology Subcommittee joint hearing on Y2K issues for the Defense Department and national security systems; March 9, the two House Subcommittee's joint hearing on Y2K liability issues. The following hearings are planned: March 22, House Government Management, Information, and Technology hearing on Y2K emergency management preparations; and March 25, Senate Y2K Committee hearing on Russian nuclear issues and U.S. plans for early warning system cooperation.

On February 24, the Senate Y2K Committee released a report summarizing the Committee's findings to date, detailing concerns with industry and service sectors that might be of greatest risk, and ranking foreign countries in terms of their Y2K preparedness. On February 22, Representative Horn released grades to federal agencies on their progress on Y2K conversion, giving an overall C+ to the federal government (his highest grade to date). On March

8, Representative Markey and Senator Harkin sponsored a nuclear Y2K symposium to investigate Y2K issues for U.S. and foreign nuclear weapons and reactors.

Recent Administration actions include: considering using some of the emergency Y2K funds from the appropriated $3.35 billion to provide assistance to resolve Y2K problems at nuclear reactor facilities in Russia and other former Soviet countries; meeting with Canada and Mexico on February 23-24 to discuss cross-border Y2K issues; announcing a second national small business action week for March 29-April 2; establishing a Y2K Help Center to provide technical support to small business at the National Institute of Standards and Technology; planning an emergency coordination center to collect, analyze and disseminate information on problems occurring in January 2000; and plans to develop a "toolkit" of information for local community use.

On March 18, the Office of Management and Budget released its eighth Quarterly Report on federal agency progress on Y2K conversion. The report states that 79% of federal mission critical systems are now Y2K compliant, and that three agencies (down from five) are not making adequate progress in their Y2K conversion efforts. The updated total cost for Y2K conversion is estimated at $6.8 billion.

BACKGROUND AND ANALYSIS

For over three years, Members and committees of Congress have helped focus national attention on the year 2000 (Y2K) computer problem, the inability of many computer systems to process dates correctly beyond December 31, 1999. The problem results from a common design scheme for computers in which dates are stored and processed using only the last two digits for the year field (e.g., 98 for 1998). The two-digit year field is very common among older systems designed when memory storage was more expensive, but it is also used in many systems built recently. With this format the year 2000 is indistinguishable from 1900. The year data-field in computer programs can perform various functions such as calculating age, sorting information by date, and comparing dates. When years beyond 1999 are entered in the two-digit format, those functions will often fail to operate properly.

While correcting a single year field is technically simple, the process of analyzing, correcting, testing, and integrating software and hardware among all computer systems that must interact is a very complex management task. In most cases, it is too expensive to purchase a completely new system, and the software must be modified to accommodate four-digit years or to incorporate some other interim solution. To determine whether a computer system needs to be modified, all of its software must be reviewed, which in some cases entails reading millions of lines of code. The process of reading and interpreting the code is made more difficult by the many computer languages in use and the shortage of programmers with skills in older languages. In addition, many older programs no longer have the accompanying documentation, such as source code (text-files of computer language instructions written by programmers). Source code cannot be directly executed, but must be compiled into object code that cannot be translated back into source code.

A further complication is that there is no single solution to correct computer systems of the Y2K problem. Rather, there are dozens of standards, public and proprietary, for storing and processing dates in computers. Also, the year 2000 is a special leap year that only occurs every 400 years to keep the calendar accurate. (Leap years occur every 4 years except years divisible by 100. However, century years are leap years if they are divisible by 400, such as 2000.) Products that are designed incorrectly will not account for the extra day needed in the year 2000. As analysts investigated the Y2K problem, other date-related problems have been identified that must be corrected to prevent computer system failures. Other dates expected to be vulnerable to computer failures include the beginning of fiscal year 2000 for many states and foreign countries, and September 9, 1999 (read 9999), which was commonly used by software programmers to indicate the termination of a function.

Many managers initially doubted the seriousness of this problem, assuming that an easy technical solution would be developed. Despite concerns that industry was exaggerating the situation, the vast majority of research has refuted this view, concluding that inspecting all computer systems, converting date fields where necessary, and then testing modified software will be very time-consuming and costly. Research firms predict that, due to a lack of time and resources, the majority of U.S. businesses and government agencies will not be able to fix all of their computer systems by January 1, 2000. The Gartner Group, an information technology research firm, estimated a cost of $30 billion to correct the problem in federal agencies and up to $600 billion worldwide. Most agencies and businesses have come to understand the difficulties involved, but some smaller firms have not yet started implementing changes. Many companies offer Y2K conversion services, and software analysis products are readily available to assist with finding and converting flawed software. While software tools can assist in solving the problem, however, most of the work must be done by humans. Some are concerned over a possible shortage of skilled programmers to perform the work, although that situation has not been widely reported.

The widespread reliance on computer systems by federal, state, and local governments, and by the private sector, raises the level of urgency for solving the problem for all systems in use. Even if the problem is corrected for a given computer system, interactions with other systems that are not Y2K compliant could result in false information corrupting the corrected database. Flawed data can enter from the private sector into government agencies' databases, and from foreign countries into U.S. computer systems. Testing is particularly laborious because the modified software must be tested in conjunction with all possible combinations of other software programs with which it interacts, to ensure that functioning has not changed. As a result of difficulty convincing executive management that this problem needed to be addressed, many companies and agencies may not be able to complete their software conversion and testing by January 1, 2000. For systems that process dates into the future, there is even less time. Many Y2K computer errors have already occurred. For additional information on media coverage of the Y2K problem see CRS Report 98-781, Year 2000 Computer Problem: Selected Internet Addresses; and CRS Report 98-994, Year 2000

Computer Problem: Selected References.

The Y2K problem exists in computer software as well as hardware components called integrated circuits (ICs), or chips, store or process data. ICs are sometimes pre-programmed or "hard-wired" by the manufacturer to store or process year data using only two digits, producing the same errors as the software that controls large computer systems when processing dates beyond 1999. ICs are used in all computer hardware (PCs, minis, and mainframes) and in many electronic devices that are not typically considered computers. Some of these "embedded chips," such as the read-only-memory (ROM), are used to store data. Other embedded chips, called microprocessors, are used to control many different types of systems such as industrial machinery, thermostats, lighting, sprinklers, medical equipment and devices, building security systems, telephone services, electric power grids, public transit systems, and other utility distribution systems.

Although most ICs do not store or process dates, those that do must be inspected and replaced, if necessary, to avoid malfunctions from Y2K incompatibility. (For the case of ROMs, some can be reprogrammed by the user to handle four digit years, but others must be physically removed and replaced with Y2K compliant ROMs.) Billions of ICs are produced and sold globally each year, leading to the possibility that great damage could result even if only a tiny fraction of them malfunction. Furthermore, ICs are produced by hundreds of different companies, some of which are located overseas. Even some ICs being produced today and embedded in other systems, may not be Y2K compliant.

Federal Efforts

Federal agencies maintain many computer systems that manage large databases, conduct electronic monetary transactions, and control numerous interactions with other computer systems. For well over a year (and in some cases for many years) federal agencies have been converting their systems to achieve Y2K compliance. **Time constraints have forced** agencies to focus on fixing only the highest priority, or "mission critical" systems, and to shift resources from other projects to work on Y2K efforts. In 1995, the Office of Management and Budget (OMB) established an interagency committee, led by the Social Security Administration, to facilitate federal efforts. These include the General Services Administration (GSA) requirement that vendor software listed in federal procurement schedules be Y2K compliant, and the National Institute of Standards and Technology (NIST) recommendation that four-digit year fields be used for any federal electronic data exchange (Federal Information Processing Standard 4-1). NIST has also developed specifications for use in testing date and time functions of computer systems for Y2K compliance.

The interagency committee developed a world-wide web site to provide information on Y2K conversion activities [http://www.itpolicy.gsa.gov/mks/yr2000/y201toc1.htm]. This web site, managed by GSA, is linked to other federal agency Y2K web sites and those of non-federal organizations that discuss activities and available resources on Y2K conversion. The committee also developed a "best practices" report, describing how agencies can best implement a solution. The report includes a comprehensive conversion plan, setting milestones for federal agency progress up to January 1, 2000, and provides a method for dividing Y2K conversion activities into five phases: 1) awareness — gaining executive level support and sponsorship; 2) assessment—conducting an inventory of core business areas and processes that could be affected by the problem and prioritizing their conversion or replacement; 3) renovation—converting, replacing, or eliminating systems, applications, databases, and interfaces; 4) validation—testing converted systems applications or databases for performance and functionality; and 5) implementation—testing for interoperability and formal acceptance, and developing contingency plans. These five phases were adopted by federal agencies and the General Accounting Office as a way of measuring progress toward correcting the problem. Much of the private sector has adopted the five phase terminology, as well as other information disseminated by the interagency committee.

In December 1996, OMB designated the interagency committee as an official subcommittee of the newly established Council of Chief Information Officers (CIOs). Through that subcommittee, the Federal Acquisitions Regulation (FAR) was amended to increase awareness of Y2K procurement issues and to ensure that solicitations and contracts address Y2K issues. The amendment has helped federal agencies to purchase Y2K compliant products by providing a uniform approach toward solutions and a single definition for compliance. In August 1997, the Federal Acquisition Regulation council adopted a final rule for Y2K purchases, requiring federal agencies to purchase systems that process all dates correctly. Noncompliant products must be upgraded by vendors before the earliest date at which they will fail to process dates correctly. However, systems will not be expected to produce correct results if corrupted data is used as the input.

The Department of Defense (DOD) has a particularly difficult challenge in inspecting, correcting, and testing all of its systems. With each military service and defense agency maintaining its own computer systems for military operations, acquisitions, and personnel functions, DOD originally took a decentralized approach to managing the Y2K problem. In 1998, however, a single individual was appointed to manage all DOD Y2K conversion efforts. DOD has several unique concerns apart from other federal agencies, such as its weapon systems that contain embedded chips that store two-digit dates, and its huge volume of computer-driven systems. With over one third of all computers in the federal government, DOD has identified 2,581 mission critical systems, 48% of which were not yet Y2K compliant as of November 15, 1998. Another problem caused by the inability of a DOD system to process dates has been found in its Global Positioning System (GPS), a satellite system that provides position and velocity information for many military and civilian aircraft (including missiles), and ground vehicles. Malfunctioning of GPS (which could occur on August 22, 1999, when the system clock resets) could cause a loss of control of these vehicles and systems.

In March 1997, at the prompting of the President's National Security Telecommunications Advisory Committee (NSTAC), the National Communications System (NCS) initiated a study of the impact of the Y2K problem on the nation's telecommunications infrastructure. NCS is a cooperative effort made up of 23 federal agencies, led by the Defense Information Systems Agency. Its mission is to coordinate national security and emergency preparedness telecommunications during any crisis or disaster. NCS is working with the telephone industry in studying the Y2K problem for public communications networks. NCS is working with the intelligence community to address these concerns and has not released further findings to the public.

As a result of increasing attention on the embedded chip problem, in May 1997, the Y2K Subcommittee formed a subgroup on medical devices and scientific equipment. The subgroup is chaired by the Department of Health and Human Services and has representatives from DOD, Food and Drug Administration, Centers for Disease Control, National Institutes of Health, Departments of Veterans Affairs, Agriculture, Justice, and the Nuclear Regulatory Commission. Their goal is to ensure that government-sponsored research and patient care are uninterrupted by Y2K problems. In January 1998, the subgroup sent a letter to over 16,000 manufacturers of medical and scientific products used by the government, to collect data on the Y2K compliance of their products. Over 1900 of those companies are manufacturers of equipment with computer components. Many of those companies still have not provided information on their products. The subgroup continues to collect additional information on medical devices and scientific equipment, and maintains a database of Y2K compliance status of products on its web site (www.fda.gov/cdrh/yr2000).

In February 1998, the President issued a directive requiring federal agencies to assure that critical federal programs are not disrupted by the Y2K problem. The directive established a Council on Y2K Conversion, led by a presidential appointee, John Koskinen (former Deputy Director of OMB), to oversee activities of all federal agencies, act as chief spokesman for the executive branch, coordinate with state, local, and tribal governments, international groups, and the private sector, and identify resources needed for agencies' Y2K conversion efforts. This appointment of a "Y2K Czar" represented a shift in Administration policy from a decentralized approach for the Y2K effort, to a more centralized management approach, as recommended by Members of Congress.

On July 14, 1998, President Clinton and Vice President Gore addressed the nation on the Y2K problem, citing several Administration initiatives underway to address the problem. These included a campaign by the Small business Administration to raise awareness among small businesses, the so-called "good Samaritan" legislation to promote information sharing in the private sector, a Department of Labor job bank for Y2K workers, a $12 million contribution to the World Bank's Y2K program, and a national campaign by the President's Y2K Council. The legislation, amended and later named the Year 2000 Information and Readiness Disclosure Act, was enacted as P.L.105-271 on October 19, 1998.

The Administration has taken several actions this year, including introducing a new toll-free telephone number (888-USA-4-Y2K) to provide Y2K information to consumers, and creating a Senior Advisors Group of chief executive officers of major companies and trade associations to provide Y2K information to the public. With requests from several Members of Congress, on January 19 President Clinton discussed the seriousness of the Y2K problem in his State of the Union address, urging all businesses and government agencies at federal, state, and local levels to work diligently toward resolving it. The President's budget request, submitted February 2, included a total of $433 million for Y2K remediations at federal agencies for FY 2000. The President's Y2K Council has identified individuals to represent each of 24 sectors of the Senior Advisors Group, which will provide updates to the Administration on the Y2K preparedness of their respective industries. The Y2K Council also established an International Y2K Cooperation Center to coordinate regional and sectoral efforts to address the Y2K problem.

State and Local Efforts

The status of Y2K remediations of state, county, and municipal governments varies widely, with many having made estimates of the costs anticipated to correct the Y2K problem for their own systems, and others not yet having completed inventories of their computer systems. In December 1996, the National Association of State Information Resource Executives (NASIRE) held a Y2K symposium, at which only 28 states were represented.
Since then, awareness and information sharing on the Y2K problem by state governments has increased markedly. NASIRE continues to monitor Y2K conversion efforts of state governments, and provides detailed information on its web site (www.nasire.org/year2000). A November 1998 report by the General Accounting Office (GAO) stated that failure by states to complete Y2K conversions could result in billions of dollars of federal benefits payments not being delivered. Some states (e.g. Nevada, Virginia, Georgia, Hawaii) have enacted laws providing full or limited immunity to the state from liability for date related computer errors, and other states are considering similar legislation.

Many city and county government Y2K efforts lag behind state and federal agencies. Federal agencies are concerned because they often receive data directly from city and county offices. For example, local police forces regularly provide information to the Department of Justice, and local health departments send information to the Department of Health and Human Services. If city or county computer systems are not Y2K compliant, they could send corrupted data to federal databases. If solutions implemented for a local computer system are incompatible with solutions implemented for a given federal system, the data transmission may fail. Cities and counties also share electronic information among themselves and with states. Incompatibility between any of these systems can lead to system failures. A survey by the National Association of Counties, released December 8, 1998, stated that half of the nation's counties do not have Y2K strategic plans, and estimated that America's counties (not including cities or towns) will spend $1.7 billion to achieve Y2K compliance. Many local groups are conducting "town hall" meetings to discuss potential problems and contingency plans at the city and community levels.

Private Sector Efforts

Major industry sectors must coordinate their efforts to correct their computer systems to insure that these sectors continue to function smoothly. The finance industry is particularly critical because it relies on many daily transactions across geographic and political boundaries. Banks, thrift savings institutions, credit unions, and stock markets must be sure that their transactions can interoperate accurately. Other industries that must coordinate their Y2K efforts include insurance companies, telecommunications providers (Federal Communications Commission web site at [http://www.fcc.gov/year2000]), utilities companies (web site on electric utilities industry at [http://www.euy2k.com]), computer manufacturers, and airlines. Many of those groups have been reluctant to discuss the Y2K status of their computer systems because of concerns over potential liability and a loss of trust by consumers. This situation may change with the recently enacted Year 2000 Information Readiness and Disclosure Act (P.L. 105-271). According to estimates, companies are spending a significant portion of their information technology budgets on Y2K conversion. Scores of companies have emerged offering software tools or services to work on the Y2K problem. Some are new consulting firms specializing in Y2K conversion, while others are established software firms that have entered this potentially lucrative business. Nevertheless, a potential shortage of available, skilled software programmers could raise the cost for Y2K conversion services as the year 2000 approaches. The Information Technology Association of America, representing the information services industry, has a Y2K certification program to evaluate the processes and methods of companies developing products and services or performing Y2K conversions. No organization has offered to evaluate the Y2K compliance of specific software or hardware products. Industry analysts are particularly concerned about small and medium-sized businesses, many of which do not have enough staff to renovate and test all internal computers and develop contingency plans for alternate suppliers and business partners.

International Efforts

Researchers agree that most foreign companies and governments lag behind those in the United States in addressing the Y2K problem. Except perhaps in Canada, the United Kingdom, Australia, and a few other countries, the issue has not received as much attention as it has in this country. With the international economy increasingly reliant on electronic commerce, U.S. businesses and government agencies have an interest in ensuring that their foreign counterparts are addressing the problem. Concern is mounting that some foreign banks are not preparing adequately to correct their systems. The European Union's decision to introduce its common currency, the euro, beginning in 1999 required financial institutions to upgrade their computer systems to handle the new currency, causing additional delay in their Y2K conversion efforts. A thorough assessment is lacking on the status of the Y2K problem in foreign countries and the potential risks for U.S. citizens and organizations, although some private sector studies are available.

In June 1997, NIST sponsored an International Symposium on the Y2K problem, intended to bring together industries and governments to discuss strategies for managing the problem, and areas of possible international coordination. Representatives from only four other countries attended the conference (Britain, Canada, Australia, and Sweden). Later in 1997, GSA attempted to raise international awareness of the problem by conducting a survey of countries to determine their level of preparedness and identify common concerns. Only two countries responded to the survey. In 1998 GSA sponsored an international Y2K "virtual conference" in which GSA received analyses and status reports of some countries, and posted reports on its web site.

Several international organizations are now involved in raising awareness of the Y2K problem. These include the United Nations (UN), the Organization for Economic Cooperation and Development, the Bank for International Settlements, the World Bank, and the European Commission, whose Y2K web sites are all linked to GSA's web site. In May 1998, the Summit of eight industrialized nations (Britain, France, Germany, Italy, Japan, Canada, United States, and Russia), discussed the Y2K problem in the context of promoting sustainable growth and political stability in the global economy. The group agreed to work with businesses and international organizations to assist developing countries in addressing the problem. On December 11, 1998, Y2K coordinators representing over 120 nations met at the UN to discuss ways to work together on common problems.

Activity in Previous Congresses

The 104 and 105th Congresses focused on prompting federal agencies, state, local and th foreign governments, and businesses to work on correcting the problem for their computer systems. (For a detailed chronology of congressional hearings and legislation, see CRS Report 98-377, Year 2000 Problem: Chronology of Hearings and Legislation, updated regularly.) These hearings, speeches, reports, and legislation have helped to increase media coverage of the Y2K issue and encourage action toward remediation.

The first congressional hearing on the Y2K problem was held in April 1996 by the House Government Oversight and Reform Committee, Subcommittee on Government Management, Information and Technology. The hearing focused on Y2K conversion issues for federal agencies. In May 1996 the House Science Committee, Subcommittee on Technology, conducted a hearing on potential technical solutions and possible roles for government in addressing the problem. These hearings revealed that major federal departments were still in initial planning stages, many agencies did not yet have cost estimates, and most agencies had not completed inventories of their code or developed plans to solve the problem. The two subcommittees began conducting joint hearing to investigate various aspects of the Y2K problem.

The 104th Congress enacted three legislative provisions regarding the Y2K problem. The FY1997 Defense

Authorization Act (P.L. 104-201) directed DOD to assess risks caused by the Y2K problem, and urged DOD to purchase only Y2K compliant products. To avoid contract delays, DOD could purchase noncompliant products if vendors made them compliant at reasonable cost. The FY1997 Omnibus Appropriations Act (P.L. 104-208) gave DOD $5 million to validate tools and methodologies for Y2K conversion. The FY1997 Treasury, Postal Service, and General Government Appropriations bill (P.L. 104-208) directed OMB to provide a cost estimate for Y2K work, a strategy to ensure that computer systems will operate in the year 2000, and a timetable for implementing the strategy.

Early in the 105 Congress, OMB submitted a report to Congress, to fulfill the th requirements of P.L. 104-208, with $2.3 billion as its first estimate of the cost to convert the software of all federal computer systems to enable the processing of dates beyond 1999. The estimate did not include upgrades or replacements of systems that would otherwise occur as part of the normal systems life cycle, or the federal share of the costs for state information systems that support federal programs. Federal agencies focused on systems they considered "mission critical" rather than all systems. The Administration's strategy was for the CIO of each agency to address the problem for their respective organizations, noting that no single approach can be taken for all systems. Attention the Y2K problem increased, however, with GAO's February 1997 report identifying the Y2K problem as a "high risk" for federal agencies, and recommending a process for agencies to achieve Y2K compliance.

In February 1997, the Senate Committee on Banking, Housing and Urban Affairs requested status information on the finance industry from the six financial regulatory agencies: the Federal Reserve Board (FRB), the Federal Deposit Insurance Corp. (FDIC), the Office of Thrift

Supervision (OTS), the National Credit Union Administration (NCUA), the Office of the Comptroller of Currency (OCC), and the Securities and Exchange Commission (SEC). The Committee obtained information on the supervisory efforts of these agencies to ensure the Y2K readiness of the financial industry. Shortly after the Committee inquiry, the Federal Financial Institutions Examination Council, an interagency body made up of the FRB, FDIC, OTS, NCUA, and OCC, issued guidelines for financial institutions and federal examiners to address to avoid major service disruptions. As a result of efforts of the House and Senate Banking Committees, the six financial regulatory agencies began providing quarterly briefings to Congress on the status of the finance industry. In March 1998, the Examination Parity and Year 2000 Readiness for Financial Institutions Act (P.L. 105-164) was enacted to extend the authority of the Office of Thrift Supervision and the National Credit Union Administration to examine the operations of service corporations or other entities that perform services under contract for thrifts and credit unions, thereby giving those agencies statutory parity with the other financial regulatory agencies.

In March 1997 the House Subcommittee on Government Management, Information and Technology and Subcommittee on Technology conducted an inquiry on the Y2K vulnerability of chips used in electronic devices that are either owned, used by, or regulated by federal departments and agencies. Based on agency responses, the CIO Council agreed to form a Biomedical Subgroup of the Y2K subcommittee to study embedded chip issues in federal agencies. The CIO Council also agreed to have agencies submit quarterly reports on the status of their Y2K efforts, with updated cost estimates.

In April 1998, the Senate established a "Special Committee on the Year 2000 Technology Problem" to study the impact of the Y2K problem on the executive and judicial branches of the federal government, state governments, and private sector in the United States and abroad. In June, the House established a Year 2000 Task Force, co-chaired by Representatives Horn and Morella, to coordinate House efforts.

The Treasury, Postal Service, and General Government Appropriations Act for FY1998 (P.L. 105-61) directed OMB to report to Congress on a quarterly basis, on federal agency progress toward Y2K conversion. To date, OMB has sent seven quarterly reports to Congress on the progress of federal agency Y2K conversion efforts. OMB's cost estimate for federal agency Y2K conversion has increased steadily and is currently $6.4 billion. OMB has targeted March 31, 1999, for federal agencies to have completed the renovation, validation, and implementation phases of all Y2K conversions. The latest report (dated November 15, released December 8) categorizes the 24 largest agencies into one of three tiers based on evidence of progress in their reports: six agencies are in tier 1 for not making adequate progress; seven agencies are in tier 2 for having evidence of progress, but with concerns; and 11 agencies are in tier 3 for making satisfactory progress. Tier 1 agencies include the Departments of Defense, Energy, Health and Human Services, Transportation (in particular the Federal Aviation Administration), State, and the Agency for International Development. Of the 6,696 mission critical systems in the 24 largest agencies, 60% are Y2K compliant, 30% must still be repaired, 7% still must be replaced, and 3% must still be retired. Other government-wide issues OMB identified include, lack of independent verification and validation of Y2K compliance, lack of contingency planning, rising costs ($1 billion increase from the last quarterly report), and data exchanges with states and other entities.

Representative Horn has released several sets of grades to federal agencies, on their Y2K conversion status. The first grades, issued in July 1996, were based on reports by federal agencies on the status of their Y2K conversion programs. Subsequent grades have been based on progress made by the agencies. The most recent grades, released November 23, 1998, gave the Administration an overall grade of D.

In the final days of the 105 Congress, three additional legislative measures on the Y2K th problem were enacted. The Defense Authorization Act (P.L. 105-261), enacted October 17, prohibits DOD from purchasing for systems that are not Y2K compliant; requires DOD to report on its Y2K compliance strategy, including contingency plans; requires DOD to develop Y2K simulations for training exercises; requires DOD and CIA to report on plans for ensuring continuity of operations, and to outline agreements with foreign countries to ensure that problems with strategic systems in those countries do not pose a threat. The Y2K Information and Readiness Disclosure Act (P.L. 105-271), enacted October 19, is intended to encourage companies to disclose information on the Y2K readiness of their products and services. On October 21, the Omnibus Appropriations Act (P.L. 105-277) was enacted, which included emergency Y2K funding for federal agency conversion efforts totaling $3.35 billion. On December 18, the Senate Special Committee on the Y2K Problem held a field hearing on potential disruption of water services.

Activity in the 106th Congress

The Y2K problem continues to receive attention in hearings and legislation of the 106 th Congress. On January 15, the Senate Appropriations Committee reviewed the status of federal agencies and other issues with the Chair of the President's Y2K Council. On January 20, a hearing by the House Government Management, Information and

Technology Subcommittee and House Technology Subcommittee investigated the Y2K status of federal, state, local, and foreign governments. The Senate Commerce Committee held a hearing on February 9 to discuss whether to limit lawsuits resulting from product or system failures associated with the Y2K problem. The Senate Commerce Committee held a hearing on February 9 to discuss whether to limit lawsuits resulting from product or system failures associated with the Y2K problem. Several Y2K-related bills have also been introduced (see legislation section).

Issues for Congress

Despite extensive media coverage and many congressional hearings, some businesses and individuals still doubt the seriousness of the Y2K problem. Numerous reports by GAO, however, identify problems with systems at every federal agency reviewed, and other non-federal systems. The vast majority of private sector studies reach similar conclusions. Some economists predict a worldwide recession caused by the Y2K problem. Virtually everyone agrees that the hearings held by Congress, along with letters to agencies, press conferences, reports, and legislation, have been effective in raising awareness. Yet many also feel that federal, state, and local agencies, and businesses have not made enough progress. The 106 th Congress will likely continue the oversight of federal efforts through hearings, communication with agencies, and press releases.

In an attempt to mitigate the negative consequences of the Y2K problem, Congress has used several strategies. One was to provide additional funding to federal agencies beyond their usual information technology budgets to work on the Y2K problem. The FY1998 Supplemental Appropriations Act (P.L. 105-174, enacted May 1, 1998) added $86 million for Y2K conversion work in the Federal Aviation Administration, the Treasury Department, and the Health

Care Finance Administration. In addition, the President's FY1999 budget request included a $3.25 billion discretionary allowance for emergencies including unforeseen defense and non-defense costs, natural disasters, and expenses of the Y2K conversion. The budget request did not specify what portion of that allowance would be used for Y2K conversion, or which agencies would use it. The Omnibus Appropriations Act for FY1999 (P.L. 105-277, enacted October 21) included $3.35 billion of emergency funds for federal agency Y2K conversion efforts ($1.1 billion for DOD and $2.25 billion for all other federal agencies), to remain available until September 30, 2001. Because they were designated as emergency funds, they did not require offsetting receipts from other appropriations. OMB controls all funds for federal agencies other than DOD and legislative branch agencies, and has already allocated $1.25 billion, leaving only $1 billion for the remainder of FY1999. Some speculate that additional FY1999 federal funding for Y2K conversion may become necessary.

Another approach used by Congress was to reprogram funds for Y2K work for specific agencies determined to need additional funds. For example, the FY1998 Treasury and General Government Appropriations Act (P.L. 105-61), directed the Internal Revenue Service (IRS) to use $376.7 million from its information systems development account for century date change efforts, and reprogrammed $87 million from other IRS programs to Y2K conversion efforts. The Departments of Veterans Affairs, Housing and Urban Development, and Independent Agencies Appropriations Act for FY1998 (P.L. 105-65) reprogrammed $8 million from existing appropriations for the Veterans Benefits Administration to work on Y2K problems. The Departments of Labor Health and Human Services, and Education, and Related Agencies Appropriations Act for FY1998 (P.L. 105-78) made $183 million available from existing appropriations for the Labor Department's Labor

Unemployment Insurance program to assist states to convert their automated state employment agency systems to be Y2K compliant.

Some observers called for the more extreme measure of mandating a four digit standard for all federal electronic data exchange, modeled after the IRS policy requiring a four-digit standard for all of its transactions. Computer industry representatives, however, argued that any standard should be developed by the private sector rather than government. They also argued that there is no time for industry to develop a consensus standard, and furthermore, that a single standard would not be appropriate for all cases. Some Members suggested that Congress should do more to ensure that information technology products are Y2K compliant. Requiring Y2K compliance in products might be unrealistic, however, because it is impossible to test all of the components in a product with every possible interface to insure Y2K compliance in all applications. To help federal purchasers, as well as consumers, GSA maintains a list on its web site of commercial off-the-shelf (COTS) products for which the manufacturer has stated are Y2K compliant (using the FAR definition for Y2K compliance).

Congress is also concerned about liability issues. Some want Congress to require that companies disclose their Y2K status. Conversely, others want Congress to set limits on the liability that a company can face if it discloses Y2K vulnerabilities of its products. Several bills have already been introduced in the 106th Congress addressing these concerns. The Administration did not establish a policy to determine whether federal agencies or their contractors are responsible for damages resulting from Y2K errors, arguing that it is more important to focus on fixing the problem.

Some Members urged the SEC to require all publicly traded companies to submit Y2K compliance disclosures for new stock offerings. Many opposed such a policy, however, arguing that whether or not to require disclosure should be decided by private sector groups rather than the SEC. In May 1997, the SEC posted a statement for public discussion on the nature of disclosure made by publicly traded companies, stating that if the Y2K problem could cause "material adverse consequences," companies should provide their projected expenditures and associated uncertainties as part of their quarterly report to the SEC. In June 1997, the SEC reported to Congress that most self-regulatory organizations (such as the stock exchanges) are making adequate progress on the Y2K problem. The SEC continued to monitor efforts of regulated entities (brokers, dealers, agents, and investment companies) and the Securities Industry Association. SEC rules require public companies to report in-house Y2K conversion costs as an expense, rather than capitalized over a period of years.

In November 1997, Senator Bennett introduced a bill (S. 1518) to direct the SEC to require all publicly traded corporations to make specific disclosures in their offering statements and quarterly reports regarding the ability of their computer systems to operate after January 1, 2000. Many businesses opposed the bill because their insurance providers would not cover damages resulting from Y2K problems, and it would be difficult to estimate their litigation costs (which was required by the bill). In January 1998, the SEC issued additional guidance to strengthen the requirements for public companies to disclose the status of their Y2K conversion efforts. After receiving the second quarterly reports with little increase in Y2K reporting, the SEC started unequivocally requiring Y2K readiness reporting, and prosecuting companies that failed to report their Y2K readiness. For further discussion, see CRS Report 98-966, The Year 2000 Computer Problem: Legal Issues.

Many Members are concerned about the efforts of foreign and international organizations to address the Y2K problem. Unless the problem is corrected within every country, both in government and the private sector, international commerce could be adversely affected. Research indicates that most of the rest of the world lags behind the United States in addressing the problem, although there is a lack of information or analysis on efforts in some countries. Some are concerned over whether foreign air traffic control systems will interoperate with U.S. systems after Y2K renovations are performed. Potential risks to safety systems of foreign nuclear energy reactors has also come into question.

Some countries, however, have strong Y2K programs in place. The British government's Action 2000 program in 1998 received £17 million for outreach and publicity, £70 million to help small and medium sized businesses address the Y2K problem, and £10 million to the World Bank to assist the Y2K conversion efforts of lesser developed countries. In FY1999 appropriations, the United States provided $12 million to the World Bank's outreach effort to lesser developed countries.

Many have become concerned over the national security implications of the Y2K problem. The possibility of a weakened command, control, communications, and intelligence (C4I) infrastructure due to potential system failures, the diversion of resources away from information security efforts, and the possible sabotage of defense systems by individuals performing Y2K remediation, are all potential risks faced by military and intelligence operations. In addition, there is concern over the continued interoperability of U.S. systems with those of NATO allies and the proper functioning Russia's early warning systems. DOD officials are discussing these issues with NATO and Russian counterparts for collaborative operations and the sharing of data. The intelligence community is also investigating the potential impact of non-compliant systems in foreign countries on U.S. systems. Reports of the Administration's activities in this area, however, are not open to the public.

Congress has become increasingly concerned over potential risks posed by the Y2K problem to critical national infrastructures, such as utilities, telecommunications, transportation, financial services, and health care. For further discussion of this issue, see CRS Report 98-967, Year 2000 Problem: Potential Impacts on National Infrastructures. The President's Y2K Council has been working with the federal agencies that regulate sectors of the economy to help the critical infrastructures in achieving Y2K compliance. Legislation was introduced in the 105th Congress requiring the Y2K Council to produce an assessment of the Y2K problem and a strategy to ensure that critical services will remain intact. On January 7, 1999, the Y2K Council issued its First Quarterly Summary of Assessment Information compiled by federal agencies. The report concludes that there will not be large-scale disruptions in key infrastructures, that the financial industry is especially well prepared, but that international failures are likely. Most of the data in the report, however, was compiled by industry groups and may not provide enough independent observation or analysis to evaluate the risks to the nation's critical services and infrastructures. In April, the Y2K Council will provide an update to its report, with additional data.

Some argue that if larger systems are not already close to becoming Y2K compliant, the companies or agencies responsible for those systems should shift their focus from compliance efforts to developing contingency plans. Only a small number of federal agencies, and very few private sector entities, have released contingency plans to the public. The Small Business Administration is implementing an outreach program to distribute Y2K informational materials to small businesses through its web page and with partners in the banking and insurance industries. Some have called for a leader from the private sector to act as a national spokesman in prompting all of the economic sectors to work together to correct and test critical infrastructures and develop contingency plans.

The Administration is also developing an emergency preparedness plan, to be implemented by several federal agencies and led by the Federal Emergency Management Agency (FEMA). The Administration has not yet released any details, however, and some observers question whether FEMA currently has the resources to respond to a potentially large number of demands for assistance that could arise in January.

In the past, although other computer-related problems have received national attention, Congress did not become deeply involved in their solutions. Two examples are computer viruses and the information systems security. The private sector was able to address these problems with virus detection software and encryption systems to provide information security, privacy, and authenticity. It is unclear, however, whether the market alone will provide the incentive for industry and government to eradicate the Y2K problem. In the future, other systemic computer problems might arise that would elicit a response from Congress, such as adapting to a new European monetary unit (EMU) or expanding the number of digits in social security numbers or telephone area codes. To lay the groundwork for addressing future computer-related problems, Congress may consider focusing more federal research on computer reliability.

LEGISLATION

H.J.Res. 14 (Linder)

Joint Resolution to designate Monday, January 3, 2000, as the day of the observance of the New Year's Day holiday in that year. The intention was to provide an extra day for government agencies to resolve Y2K problems before commencing normal operations in the new year. Several groups, however, including the Administration, have opposed this idea, arguing that the additional software changes necessary to implement the change in holiday observance would further complicate Y2K renovations and testing. Introduced January 6, 1999; referred to Committee on Government Reform.

H.R. 179 (Thurman)
Businesses Undergoing the Glitch Act, would allow small businesses to deduct Y2K conversion costs from their gross income for federal income tax reporting. Introduced January 6, 1999; referred to Committee on Ways and Means.

H.R. 192 (Manzullo)
Year 2000 Consumer Protection Plan Act of 1999, would establish judicial and administrative proceedings, a standard of proof, and damage limitations for legal actions brought in cases of Y2K processing failures. Introduced January 6, 1999; referred to Committee on the Judiciary.

H.R. 775 (Davis)
Year 2000 Readiness and Responsibility Act, to establish procedures and limitations for civil actions brought for damages relating to the Y2K failure of any device or system. Introduced February 23, 1999; referred to Judiciary Committee.

S. 96 (McCain)
Y2K Act, would limit liability and damages for defendants in suits involving Y2K failures. Introduced January 19; referred to Committee on Commerce, Science and Transportation.

S. 174 (Moynihan)
Y2K State and Local GAP (Government Assistance Programs) Act of 1999, would provide funding for states to correct Y2K problems in computers used to administer state and local programs. Introduced January 19, 1999; referred to Committee on Finance.

S. 314 (Bond)
Small Business Year 2000 Readiness Act, to direct the Small Business Administration (SBA) to establish a loan guarantee program to address Y2K problems of small businesses at slightly higher amounts than SBA's existing 7(a) general business loan program. Introduced January 27, 1999; referred to Committee on Small Business; reported to Senate February 23 S.Rept. 106-5); passed Senate without amendment March 2; introduced in House (H.R. 1056) and referred to Small Business Committee March 3; hearing March 12.

S. 461 (Hatch)
Year 2000 Fairness and Responsibility Act, to foster an incentive to settle Y2K lawsuits that may disrupt significant sectors of the American economy by requiring procedures to be followed before and during Y2K civil actions and class actions. Introduced February 24, 1999; referred to Judiciary Committee; hearing March 1.

Appendix E - Major Initiatives in US Congress Regulatory Activities in Financial Sector

Date	Individuals/ Organizations Involved	Action	Response
1997 Feb & Apr	US Senators Bennett & D' Amato (US Senate Banking, Housing & Urban Affairs Committee, Subcommittee on Financial Services & Technology)	Cosigned letters to 6 federal financial institution regulatory agencies asking they provide info on their Y2K readiness & industry sector under their supervision.	Responses raised serious questions about Y2K readiness in financial sector. Senators decided to *hold hearings to investigate further.*
1997 Jul 10	US Senate -1st Hearing on Financial Services & Y2K (Subcommittee on Financial Services & Technology)	Subcommittee solicited testimony from Y2K experts such as Jinnett.	Issues raised would reemerge consistently throughout other hearings. Affirmed Subcommittee's conclusion that *regulators would play critical role in Y2K preparedness.*

Date	Individuals/ organizations involved	Action	Response
1997 Jul 30	Hearing - US Financial Institutions & Federal Regulatory Agencies Management of Y2K (Subcommittee on Financial Services & Technology)	As result of letters sent in Feb & Apr 1997, the heads of 6 financial institution regulatory agencies were prepared to address concerns of Subcommittee.	Most agencies started to actively engage the Y2K issue in June 1996 in response to FFIEC statement. Jul 1997 - FFIEC provided 2nd statement that provided guidance on Y2K project management. www.FFIEC.g ov/Y2K/ *Senators requested quarterly written progress reports.*

Date	Individuals/ organizations involved	Action	Response
1997 Oct 22	Hearing - The Year 2000 Liability & Disclosure (Subcommittee on Financial Services & Technology)	Solicited testimony from Y2K lawyers, president of ITAA, & investment analyst	Focus - Y2K information sharing & liability risks. SEC reiterated its position - current guidelines are sufficient to compel Y2K disclosure. Mentioned GAO report assessing NCUA Y2K compliance. Warned other regulatory agencies that GAO wold visit them soon.

Date	Individuals/ organizations involved	Action	Response
1997 Nov 4	Hearing - Mandating Y2K Disclosure by Publicly Trade Companies (Subcommittee on Financial Services & Technology)	Solicited testimony from Yardeni. Hearing was a step to pressure public companies to provide greater Y2K disclosure.	Yardeni supported need for new comprehensive disclosure law. Legislation was introduced - Y2K Computer Remediation & Shareholder (CRASH) Protection Act of 1997. (Bennett wrote Pres. Clinton about lack of national leadership in Y2K area.)

Date	Individuals/ organizations involved	Action	Response
1998 Feb 10	Hearing - FDIC's Year 2000 Preparedness (Subcommittee on Financial Services & Technology)	5th Hearing of Subcommittee provided public forum for examining results of GAO's assessment of FDIC's Y2K efforts. FDIC lagged behind OMB & GAO guidelines.	(Pres. Clinton created President's Council on Y2K Conversion) Subcommittee discussed shutdown date for noncompliant institutions & need to provide customers with meaningful disclosure on their banks' Y2K readiness.

Date	Individuals/ organizations involved	Action	Response
1998 Feb 18	Field hearing implications of the Y2K (Subcommittee on Financial Services & Technology)	Senator Dodd chaired 6th hearing in Hartford, Connecticut to illustrate breadth & pervasiveness of Y2K problem. 7 witnesses described their Y2K programs & implications for customers.	Participants reaffirmed interdependent nature of business & encouraged consumers to ask their product & service providers about their Y2K efforts. Legislation was introduced - Examination Parity & Y2K readiness for Financial Institutions Act.

147

Date	Individuals/ organizations involved	Action	Response
1998 Mar 18	Hearing - Office of Thrift Supervision (OTS) Y2K Preparedness (Subcommittee on Financial Services & Technology)	OTS was criticized for not having completed its contingency plans & ignoring the interrelationships between its internal systems.	OTS estimated less than 22% of its regulated institutions needed improvement & around 1% were unsatisfactory in their Y2K efforts. (April, Senate voted establish new committee Special Committee on Y2K)

Date	Individuals/ organizations involved	Action	Response
1998 Jun 10	Hearing - Disclosing Year 2000 Readiness (Subcommittee on Financial Services & Technology)	SEC reported on progress of its efforts to improve Y2K disclosure among publicly traded enterprises. Triaxsys Research provided results from survey of Y2K disclosure of publicly held companies.	(April - Legislation was introduced). Corporations have violated SEC guideline requiring specifics rather than boilerplates disclosures. Hearing finished with debate on pros & cons of providing liability protection to corporate boards & senior management.
1998 Jul 6	Field Hearing - Assessing the Y2K Preparedness of Foreign Countries & Determining Just Where & How the US May be Vulnerable	Members from US financial services confirmed that intl. preparedness poses a real risk.	Witnesses mentioned international efforts such as the Joint Year 2000 Council.
1998 Sep	Hearing - Y2K & Pensions & Mutual	Fund managers efforts to	Committee wanted to

| 17 | Funds | address Y2K. | ensure analysts recognized Y2K as important risk. |

The data are extracted from the US Congress report "Investigating the Impact of the Year 2000 Problem" (1999, p80).

Appendix F - Sample Knowledge Creation Process for Shell *(Period 3 1997 - 1999 Aug)*

Needs of Enterprise	Y2K Team	Source	Sense Making	Due Diligence	Intellectual Capital (IC) (Knowledge)
What is really the problem?		Y2K Survival Guide	Approach from business survival perspective (Metaphor: The Titanic)	Consultancy report	Y2K risk assessment
What would happen if Shell does nothing? What is risk?		Shell's Year 2000 Survival (p1, p27)	Change management.	Consultancy report	Y2K risk assessment

Appendix F - Sample Knowledge Creation

Needs of Enterprise	Y2K Team	Source	Sense Making	Due Diligence	Intellectual Capital (IC) (Knowledge)
What must be done?		Shell's Year 2000 Survival (p1) (Management issue must be approached with high priority). Set up steering committee.	Not just an IT problem but embraces industrial automation & the business chain	Steering Committee of senior managers with defined terms of reference & minute of meetings	Y2K risk assessment
Who bears responsibility?	Year 2000 project manager	Y2K Survival Guide (General Manager is responsible.) Recommend: appoint Year 2000 Project Manager	Can management manage uncertainty against a fixed non-negotiable deadline?	Justification of appointment of project manager	Project manager justification within context of potential crisis

Appendix F - Sample Knowledge Creation

Needs of Enterprise	Y2K Team	Source	Sense Making	Due Diligence	Intellectual Capital (IC) (Knowledge)
What does it all involve?		Y2K Survival Guide (Using project management approach, project should be phased, include inventory, impact analysis, conversion, testing & implementation)	Phased approach (Figure 12);	Phased methodology - procedure	Phased methodology modified for multinational enterprise in oil industry

Appendix F - Sample Knowledge Creation

Needs of Enterprise	Y2K Team	Source	Sense Making	Due Diligence	Intellectual Capital (IC) (Knowledge)
How long?		Y2K Survival Guide (Everything with an IT component needs to be checked &, if necessary, corrected & tested).	Time management	Outline timetable & tasks	Establishing programs to implement based on timetable

Appendix F - Sample Knowledge Creation

Needs of Enterprise	Y2K Team	Source	Sense Making	Due Diligence	Intellectual Capital (IC) (Knowledge)
What are the key challenges to tackle?	Applications development manager; Operations manager; Technical programming manager; Database manager; Production manager; Facilities engineer; Purchasing manager;	Y2K Survival Guide (appoint Project manager; ensure entire enterprise understands; appoint sub-project (domain) project managers; monitor & manage progress; track external exposures in business chain; manage public response;	Project management (deJager & Bergeon, p25)	Project management - procedures, roles,	Roles of project management team

	Security officer; Public relations manager			
What is recommended project plan?	Y2K Survival Guide (timetable of: Phase I Inventory, Phase II Remedial Action Planning, Phase III Testing & Implementation)	Project management	Project Plan	Project Plan based on Phase I, II, III
How do we begin addressing the problem?	Y2K Survival Guide (Initiation Plan)	Project management	Initiation Plan; Health Checklist - for getting started	Activities associated - Initiation Plan

Appendix F - Sample Knowledge Creation

Needs of Enterprise	Y2K Team	Source	Sense Making	Due Diligence	Intellectual Capital (IC) (Knowledge)
What is the scope of the problem?		Y2K Survival Guide Consider areas: infrastructure, applications, communications, end-user computing, automation in physical operations; management issues		Project Plan -task, reporting & monitoring activities	Project Plan

Appendix F - Sample Knowledge Creation

Needs of Enterprise	Y2K Team	Source	Sense Making	Due Diligence	Intellectual Capital (IC) (Knowledge)
How can we find out more about Y2K problem?		Y2K Survival Guide (Conferences, articles, reports, letters, web sites such as vendors, associations, etc.)	Information seeking via personal contact, professional associations, database search, etc.	Approach - for finding additional information such as Internet, library & Intranet searching	External explicit information on Y2K
What guideline should we adopt company wide/		Y2K Survival Guide (Issue Letter from CEO; Year 2000 Guidelines)		Letter from CEO to all staff; Year 2000 Guidelines	Enterprise's approach

Appendix F - Sample Knowledge Creation

Needs of Enterprise	Y2K Team	Source	Sense Making	Due Diligence	Intellectual Capital (IC) (Knowledge)
What can internal audit review?	Auditor	Y2K Survival Guide (Determine what is needed to meet regulatory changes; develop process monitor changes to data; review progress of Y2K compliance)		Internal audit review. Overview of Y2K Risk. Risk assessment report.	

Appendix F - Sample Knowledge Creation

Needs of Enterprise	Y2K Team	Source	Sense Making	Due Diligence	Intellectual Capital (IC) (Knowledge)
What legal issues are there?	Lawyer	Y2K Survival Guide (Consider: Y2K compliance clauses for new contracts; compliance of vendor's products under existing contracts; compliance where services have been outsource; assist with due diligence process; liabilities and insurance; effect		Contract review process; Guidelines for Outsourcing; Recommendations for communicating with external persons such as media, public, vendors;	Outsourcing tasks and monitoring; Due Diligence approach; Review & revision of contracts;

		of local legislation; portfolio acquisitions/dispo sals) Shell's Year 2000 Survival (p49)			Integration approach
What about links in our business chain?	Third party liaison officer; Quality assurance representati ve	Y2K Survival Guide (work pro-actively with third parties (suppliers, customers, Government, etc.) to secure Y2K compliance		Vendor Compliance Letter. Integration test plan and results.	

Appendix F - Sample Knowledge Creation

Needs of Enterprise	Y2K Team	Source	Sense Making	Due Diligence	Intellectual Capital (IC) (Knowledge)
How do you conduct the inventory?		Y2K Survival Guide (Method - Rapid Initial Assessment.)	Assessment technique for scaling the problem	Rapid Initial Assessment - inventory (independent verification report)	Inventory
What are the terms of reference?		Shell's Year 2000 Survival (p7)		Standard terms of reference. BSI Definition of Y2K Compliance	Operational definition Y2K compliance
How can determine compliance?		Y2K Survival Guide (Definition of Y2K compliance)		Define and test compliance	Approach - identify & test compliance

Appendix F - Sample Knowledge Creation

Needs of Enterprise	Y2K Team	Source	Sense Making	Due Diligence	Intellectual Capital (IC) (Knowledge)
How do we choose date conversion strategy?		Shell's Year 2000 Survival (Comparison of conversion strategies)		Comparison of conversion strategies	Date conversion options
How should interfaces be taking into account?		Y2K Survival Guide (Plan to check & test all interfaces & platforms)		Integration Process. Strategy for Determining Critical Partners	Integration approach
How can we find external help?		Y2K Survival Guide (Identify resource constraints & secure additional capacity) Shell's Y2K Survival	Outsource for tools, code conversion, consultancy support	Outsource justification & guidelines. How to Analyse Your Current Relationship with Supplier.	External resources

Needs of Enterprise	Y2K Team	Source	Sense Making	Due Diligence	Intellectual Capital (IC)
		(p50)			
How should we approach testing & implementation?		Y2K Survival Guide (Test plan, should include items with "claimed compliant") Shell's Year 2000 Survival (p13)		Application test strategy template. Procedures for testing	Testing procedures, options & challenges

Appendix F - Sample Knowledge Creation

Needs of Enterprise	Y2K Team	Source	Sense Making	Due Diligence	Intellectual Capital (IC) (Knowledge)
What is a due diligence process?		Shell's Year 2000 Survival (p4). Providing an audit trail of a systematic & thorough approach to the problem, so as to strengthen eventual defenses in event of litigation.	Documentation approach	Due Diligence Process - with documented proof	Creation of Due Diligence Process
What is covered in contingency planning?		Shell's Year 2000 Survival (p51) - Establish business contingency plans		Operational contingency & crisis-response plan	Contingency & Disaster Recovery Plans

INDEX

litigation, 3, 23, 29, 40, 65, 66, 73, 74, 76, 77
Lockheed, 38
Martin, 38
Meta Group, 29
millennium bug, 5, 20, 43
million, 18, 19, 43, 54, 57, 58, 75, 76
NCB, 20, 49, 50, 54, 57
Nike, 38, 39
OMB, 20
online discussion forums, 5, 68
outsourced, 34, 78
Paul Revere, 26
Period 1, 7, 9, 79
Period 2, 7, 15, 24, 31, 34, 79
Period 3, 7, 36, 40, 42, 49, 53, 58, 60, 64, 79
phased approach, 21, 39
phases, 21, 39
preventive idea, 12
PSA, 12
repair industry, 34, 35
response model, 9
responses, 4, 7, 9, 12, 13, 22, 40, 74, 77, 79
retrospective tracing, 5
Rogers, 12, 29
Rubin, 29, 31
share information, 21
Shell, 38, 57, 58, 59, 60, 64, 68, 70
SIM, 24, 29
Simpson, 29, 73
Singapore, 1, 4, 5, 12, 20, 40, 49, 50, 51, 54, 56, 57, 77
specialists, 7, 36, 60, 79
SPG, 33
SSA, 12, 20
survey, 15, 18, 29, 30, 47, 53, 54
Tick, 32
triage, 22
UK, 1, 22, 26, 38, 40, 53, 55, 56, 57, 77
UKOOA, 38
Union Pacific, 32
US, 1, 2, 4, 9, 11, 12, 20, 26, 30, 39, 40, 42, 43, 44, 45, 49, 50, 53, 54, 55, 56, 57, 58, 66, 70, 73, 74, 76, 77
vendors, 7, 20, 23, 30, 51, 60, 65, 66, 75, 78
warnings, 9, 12, 13
web, 2, 5, 21, 26, 29, 31, 32, 33, 58, 60, 61, 62, 63, 67, 68, 73, 74
webiometrics, 5
windowing, 19, 35
World Bank, 3, 22, 31, 56, 57, 63, 78
Y2K problem, 1, 3, 4, 5, 6, 19, 20, 24, 30, 34, 36, 40, 42, 43, 54, 56, 58, 59, 67, 70, 73, 75, 78, 79, 80